The moral curriculum: a sociological analysis

METHUEN

First published in 1978 by Methuen & Co Ltd
11 New Fetter Lane, London EC4P 4EE
© 1978 Mrs R. Musgrave
Printed in Great Britain
by Richard Clay (The Chaucer Press) Ltd
Bungay, Suffolk

ISBN (hardbound) 0 416 85600 4
ISBN (paperback) 0 416 85620 9

CONTENTS

Contemporary
sociology of
the school
General editor
JOHN EGGLESTON

The moral curriculum:
a sociological analysis

CONTEMPORARY SOCIOLOGY
OF THE SCHOOL

PAUL BELLABY
The sociology of comprehensive schooling

BRIAN DAVIES
Social control and education

SARA DELAMONT
Interaction in the classroom

JOHN EGGLESTON
The ecology of the school

ERIC HOYLE
School organization and administration

COLIN LACEY
The socialization of teachers

PETER MUSGRAVE
The moral curriculum: a sociological analysis

PHILIP ROBINSON
Education and poverty

MICHAEL STUBBS
Language, schools and classrooms

WILLIAM TYLER
The sociology of educational inequality

TOM WHITESIDE
The sociology of educational innovation

Acknowledgements

The reading, research and thinking for this book was done mainly during 1976, a year of study leave spent in Britain. I, therefore, wish to express my thanks to the following:

The Council of Monash University for granting me leave and my colleagues in the Faculty of Education at Monash for doing my duties in my absence; the Master and Fellows of Corpus Christi College, Cambridge, who elected me a Visiting Scholar for the first two terms of 1976 and made my stay so happy and worthwhile, and Professor Raymond Illsley of the Institute of Medical Sociology, Aberdeen University, who gave me a room during the third term of 1976 and who together with his colleagues gave me much sociological stimulation; the heads, staff and some pupils of the English secondary schools in which a small research project was undertaken; my wife, who besides other support, typed the research papers upon which much of this book relies.

I also wish to thank my colleague Professor R. J. W. Selleck, who made valuable comments upon a draft of this book; the editor of this series, Professor S. J. Eggleston, for some useful advice; a reader for Methuen for some helpful comments; the editors of the following journals for permission to quote from the articles indicated: *Journal of Moral Education* (Musgrave, 1976), *Cambridge Journal of Education* (Musgrave, 1977b); and Mrs C.

Stuart and Mrs V. Newson, who typed the manuscript with great efficiency.

PWM

Monash
July 1977

Editor's introduction

Sociology has changed dramatically in the past decade. Sociologists have provided an ever increasing diversity of empirical and theoretical approaches that are advancing our understanding of the complexities of societies and their educational arrangements. It is now possible to see the over-simplification of the earlier sociological view of the world running smoothly with agreed norms of behaviour, with institutions and individuals performing functions that maintained society and where even conflict was restricted to 'agreed' areas. This normative view of society with its functionalist and conflict theories has now been augmented by a range of interpretative approaches in which the realities of human interaction have been explored by phenomenologists, ethnomethodologists and other reflexive theorists. Together they have emphasized the part that individual perceptions play in determining social reality and have challenged many of the characteristics of society that the earlier sociologists had assumed to be 'given'.

The new approaches have had striking effects upon the sociology of the school. Earlier work was characterized by a range of incompletely examined assumptions about such matters as ability, opportunity and social class. Sociologists asked how working-class children could achieve in the schools like middle-class children. Now they also ask how a social system defines class, opportunities and achievement. Such concepts and many others such as subjects, the curriculum and even schools themselves are seen to be products of the social system in which they exist. In our study of the school we can now explore more fully the ways in which individual teachers' and students' definitions of their situation help to determine its social arrangements; how perceptions of achievement can not only define achievement but also identify those who achieve; how expectations about schooling can determine the very nature and evaluation of schools.

This series of volumes explores the main areas of the sociology of the school in which a new understanding of events is now available. Each introduces the reader to the new interpretations, juxtaposes them against the longer standing perspectives and reappraises the contemporary practice of education and its consequences.

In each, specialist authors develop their own analyses of central issues such as poverty, opportunity, comprehensive schooling, the language and interaction of the classroom, the teacher's role, the ecology of education, and ways in which education acts as an instrument of social control. The broad spectrum of themes and treatments is closely interrelated; it is offered to all who seek new illumination on the practice of education and to those who wish to know how contemporary sociological theory can be applied to educational issues.

A particular feature of recent developments in the sociology of the school has been the 'rediscovery' of the sociology of knowledge. What counts as valid knowledge in the school? How is it defined and evaluated? Does the availability of knowledge constitute a form of social control? At the very heart of the *corpus* of school knowledge is that which is usually labelled Moral Education. In this volume Peter Musgrave opens up this area of the curriculum for the first time with a distinctively sociological analysis. Basing his argument on his own research in the field, he explores the moral choices of children, the processes whereby they make choices, the values by which their choices are governed and the broader social factors within which those values exist. He considers how young people understand rules, responsibilities, privileges and punishments. The analysis is not only societal but also historical and the book embodies a twentieth-century social history of the moral curriculum that shows clearly how teachers have moved from their once certain views of what is right and wrong, good and bad. The new and original argument of the book, the fundamental significance of the area and the dearth of previous sociological analysis ensure that Peter Musgrave's book will be of the greatest importance for those who need to know about the state of moral education in contemporary schools.

John Eggleston

John Ingleson

1

Introduction

Children can achieve either as persons or as scholars.
(Kay, 1975, p. 353)

A curriculum may be of the traditional type that is carefully planned by a teacher or of the type at present fashionable, but uncommon, that is supposed to emerge from a process of negotiation between teacher and learner, but, as Kay indicates in the quotation that heads this chapter, in both these cases the knowledge that is learnt can be seen as either behavioural or academic in nature. In the latter case the knowledge that is transmitted is based on the academic disciplines upon which school subjects have been, and for the most part still are, founded; in the former case the knowledge relates to ways of behaving as a human being in the particular society in which the school is situated. It is with this part of the curriculum, and, as will be explained in the next chapter, more specifically with behaviour towards others that this book is concerned.

Elsewhere (Musgrave, 1973a, p. 41) the curriculum has been defined as 'those learning experiences or succession of such experiences that are purposefully arranged by formal educational organizations'. This definition restricts attention to what any school *aims* to teach and excludes those unplanned and often unconscious lessons, now often known as 'the hidden curriculum'. Thus, a school's organization through, for example, the manner in which assemblies are run, can inadvertently teach its pupils a deferential way of treating others. Such latent functions of the school will not be a major item for consideration here. The hidden curriculum will largely be ignored not because it is not important, but because there is not room in a small book to consider every aspect of the moral curriculum. The strategy adopted is that we should be wise to focus on how those in schools do what they claim they plan to do before turning to what is achieved either without conscious planning or in a Machiavellian and secret manner so that the pupils learn some way to behave without knowing that they are doing so.

The field of morals has gained far more attention from philosophers than it has from sociologists and the first step must be to see what advantages can be gained from undertaking sociological work in this field. Some social scientists have previously examined topics relating to morality. Their contributions will be examined in the next chapter. From it a number of key concepts will emerge, whose use, it is felt, will add new dimensions to the analysis of moral education. First, the process of moral choice will be seen to be a necessary central focus, but, second, the identity in any society of what will be called 'agents of respectability' will also become of major importance for the analysis.

In the third chapter the theoretical concepts chosen will be used to examine the process by which some teenagers make moral choices and the values by which these choices seem to be governed. This chapter is based on a small study undertaken in England during 1976, though comparisons with similar data relating to the early sixties can be made, thus making possible some consideration of recent changes in moral codes. Analysis of the data gathered will allow the construction of a suggested sociological framework for considering moral choice. Such a framework has not been attempted previously and even in the, perhaps, primitive form outlined here has important implications for those interested in moral education.

Many contemporary sociologists have come to put great emphasis on what used to be seen as the social-psychological aspects of their discipline, sometimes almost forgetting that individuals act within the constraints of a larger society, the structure of which has reached its present form through a process of historical development. In the fourth chapter the main ways in which moral

14

codes have developed since the turn of the century will be traced with the aim of trying to discover who had the power to control how people were supposed to behave and to discover whether past moral codes still have much influence on what is taught to-day.

To examine moral education in this way should encourage teachers to stand back from what they are doing routinely today so that they can see how they are influenced by the past. They can then more easily consider whether they wish to continue to be so influenced. In addition, and directly relevant to the last point, the analysis will have certain implications of a theoretical nature relating to the way in which codes of morality change. If teachers wish to escape from past moral influences and to teach a new version of morality to their pupils then they are more likely to succeed if they have some conceptions of moral change, even if their theories are primitive in nature.

The analysis in the fourth chapter is at the societal level, but consideration must also be given to what goes on in the schools. In the fifth chapter we shall examine the development of various elements in the moral curriculum in Britain since 1900. Attention will have to be given not only to the obvious school subjects — religious education and moral education, but to physical education, health education and such academic subjects as English and history as well as, briefly, to certain elements of school organization and to some extra-curricular elements of the moral curriculum.

Finally, as a result of the whole analysis certain conclusions will be drawn in the last chapter. An attempt will be made to answer the question how we may best in sociological terms conceptualize moral education in such a way that is helpful to those involved in dealing with children in schools. Indeed, in brief the aim here is to help the thinking of those who wish to, or have to, deal with some of the most intractible problems of contemporary education. Fundamentally, this book is a sociological consideration of the teaching of 'oughts' and 'ought nots', and can, therefore, be seen, to use the title of a recent film, ultimately to be about 'Love and death and the whole damned thing'.

2

Sociologists, morality and moral education

We define men only in relationship to involvement
(Sartre, 1947, p. 51)

Past work (Cahiers, 1964)

In general, sociologists have not made morality a main topic for consideration, though there is one major exception: Durkheim. Amongst those that have, four levels of analysis may be isolated: that at which institutions are compared cross-culturally, the institutional level in which education is considered as one major social institution, the action level and, finally, the social-psychological level.

Comparative social institutions

The early sociologists were much concerned with the way in which whole societies developed and how their various identifiable parts related to each other. They often attacked their problems by comparing a number of different societies in order to identify which particular social institutions, for example, religion, the family or the economy, influenced the rate and the manner of the development of the whole society or of some other institution within it, for example, education or the polity. These sociologists worked from the perspective of social structure and traced the way in which different social institutions functioned within various societies.

Montesquieu 'may be said to have been the first sociologist of morality, ... his theory was that every rule or social custom serves a need' (Ossowska, 1971, p. 103). In this century several sociologists have worked in the field of morals at the social-structural level, though perhaps not with such an obviously functional perspective as did Montesquieu. Hobhouse (1906) and Westermarck both used the classical method of comparing whole societies to try to show how moral systems evolved and which social institutions governed their evolution. Perhaps oddly, when one considers Hobhouse's pioneering work in comparative psychology, it was Westermarck who gave more weight to psychological considerations. He evolved the theory that 'the moral concepts, which form the predicates of moral judgment, are ultimately based on moral emotions that are essentially generalizations of tendencies in certain phenomena to call forth either indignation or approval'. (1908, II, p. 738) As this quotation implies, there was some tendency for Westermarck to focus more on individual than on social attributes. Ginsberg, originally Hobhouse's collaborator, also made substantial sole contributions in this area, as much as a social philosopher as a sociologist, for example, in his analysis of what is really meant by 'moral progress' (1947). More recently the Polish sociologist Ossowska (1971) has outlined the factors influencing moral change at the institutional level.

Gurwitch has summed up the approach and methods adopted by these writers: '... the sociology of morality is that part of the sociology of the human spirit which studies variable types of collective moral conduct as functions of social structure, ... by an interpretative understanding of the moral values actually inspiring this conduct'. (1943, p. 147) Sociologists have tended to focus on the first part of this summary so that much of their work has been in terms of the functions of social institutions and, hence, has assumed without question the goals pursued by members of the societies concerned. Such analyses can describe, but not explain, social phenomena (S. Cohen, 1968, pp. 47–64). Furthermore, as will be seen in the next chapter, the interpretative methods used by contemporary sociology appear to be more powerful than those used by the writers to whom reference has been made.

Education as an institution

Durkheim was the pioneer at this level. He examined morals in a very general way in much of his work on, for example, the division of labour, and in a more specific way in his writing on the sociology of education. In 1902 Durkheim was appointed Professor of Education and Sociology at the Sorbonne and gave a course of lectures, ultimately reprinted as *Moral Education* (1961). At that time this course was the only common requisite of all prospective teachers in French secondary schools; it was concerned with what was most important in the common elements of education, namely morality. Durkheim's aim was 'to introduce a new secular morality based on his understanding of individualism as the core value of modern society' (Bellah, 1973, p. xxxix).

Durkheim applied the approach and methods used in comparing social institutions to a study of moral education. In the first part of this work, 'The Elements of Morality', he isolated three 'fundamental elements of morality'; the first was 'the spirit of discipline' (p. 31), the double function of which was 'to promote a certain regularity in people's conduct and to provide them with determinate goals that at the same time limit their horizons' (p. 47). The second element consisted in the 'attachment to a social group' (p. 78). The final elements was 'autonomy' based (perhaps paradoxically in the eyes of some today) on 'as clear and complete awareness as possible of the reasons for our conduct' (p. 120).

In the second part of his book, 'How to Develop the Elements of Morality in the Child', Durkheim went on to apply this analysis to the organization of schools with the aim of providing moral education. He gave great attention to discipline and to the use of punishments (four and a half chapters) and less (half a chapter) to rewards. A further chapter considered attachment to groups and in two final chapters he examined specific school subjects; one of these chapters was on the sciences and the other on aesthetics and history. The sciences were of high importance to Durkheim, largely because they showed the immense and interlocking complexity of the world. Art he saw as too unconcerned with reality to be of use for moral education. History, however, was important since it 'can give the student a very adequate idea of society and the way it is linked with the individual' (p. 275).

Three key constituents of Durkheim's analysis make difficulties for its acceptance in its entirety by many sociologists today. First, there is his emphasis on authority; thus, 'morality ... constitutes a category of rules where the idea of authority plays an absolute predominant role' (p. 29). Yet, despite the contemporary distrust of authority and despite this author's predispositions when he began this work, a position that is parallel in this respect to Durkheim's will be reached in the final chapter, though by a rather different logical route. Second, he wrote that 'to act morally is to act in terms of the collective interest' (p. 59); this assumption of unity in society is hard to uphold in an age of pluralism. Third, though this comment is not really relevant in this context, his analysis is almost entirely in terms of direct teaching; very little emphasis is put upon the non-cognitive elements in moral education.

Very recently Kay (1975) has gathered a mass of empirically based data to cover much the same ground as Durkheim did but with a much greater stress on non-cognitive factors. Kay sums up his aim as to show 'the ways in which a child's personality is moulded by society, home and school' (p. 336). Since he emphasizes the transmission of sub-cultural, mainly social class, moralities he cannot be criticized for ignoring the contemporary trend to pluralism, but just because his emphasis is on the *transmission*, not the creation, of social reality the whole tone of the analysis is somewhat deterministic.

Social action

Weber is often seen as the pioneer in the interpretative analysis of social action. For Weber the actors involved in any situation were deeply influenced in what they did by their perceptions of each other, that is, by the meaning for them of the actions of all concerned. The interpretation of the meaning, not just the form, of any action is crucial for this sociological tradition. There have been two analyses of morality at the level of action, using this term in the Weberian sense. First, Mueller-Deham (1944) gave an account of 'the sociological foundations of ethics' rooted in three basic relationships – group membership, reciprocity and associations at work. In the first two cases both positive and negative relationships were posited. However, in the case of the third basic relationship a negative dimension was not adduced and nor was it clear why 'work' was isolated as a basic relationship – indeed, thirty years later in our leisure-filled society the choice is, perhaps, substantively even less justifiable.

Second, Loubser (1971) has constructed an ideal type of moral action based on the four Parsonian pattern variables. In this analysis moral action is defined as that action which is affectively neutral, stresses quality not performance, is universal and is diffuse. There are two problems implicit in this way of formulating morality. First, some action, for example, art criticism, is categorized as 'moral' by this ideal type when actors in our culture would not themselves categorize it in that way. Second, moral concepts, as McIntyre (1967a) has shown, themselves change through time, so that the ideal type here isolated probably does not have the universality apparently presumed.

Despite the criticisms made of these two versions of the social action approach we shall build on the work of Mueller-Deham because he defined morality more carefully than most of those who have worked in this field. Also, there are certain broad parallels, and even lines of indirect influence, between the Weberian way of interpreting social action and that of Schutz whose work will be central to the analysis of the next chapter.

Social psychology

Two traditions of work are here relevant. There is a certain amount of empirical work by psychologists, particularly concerned with moral attitudes, for example, E. M. and E. Eppel (1966), but also showing how those concerned see the various aspects of school life contributing to the moral education of students (McPhail *et al.*, 1972). In addition, some social psychologists have surveyed the field in a way that provokes interesting questions. Thus, Harding (1953, p. 48) has asked, 'Where do we get our standards?' and 'Why do we try to behave morally?' Answers to questions such as these, as will be seen in Chapter 4, are usually most easily reached through a sociological, rather than a social-psychological, approach; that is, analysis must be directed towards the way in which the social situation is structured rather than towards the view taken by individuals of that structure.

Until the mid-1960s the sociological attack on such problems focussed on the concept of role. Usually this was linked to what philosophers see as the ethical domain by positing that behaviour in a specific role was governed by norms specifying what should or should not be said or done. Scott (1971) has emphasized the part played by the sanctions that are brought to bear to ensure that role players behave as is expected of them. Emmet (1966) has examined the relationship between ethics and sociology from this standpoint. She wrote, 'the notion of *role* ... provides a link between factual descriptions of social situations and moral pronouncements about what ought to be done in them' (p. 41). Yet, though Emmet clearly saw that 'moral decisions have to be made in situations' (p. 138) her conception of role is somewhat, though not entirely (see p. 149), deterministic, as can be seen in her heavy emphasis on roles in organizations and on role morality in the traditional professions. Another important objection to the use of the concept of role concerns the fact that there tends to be an assumption that most of those occupying a particular social position, e.g. of teacher, will play the role as expected, whereas we know that the tolerated range of behaviour in any such position is very great.

To conclude this introductory section four points will be made:

1 As may have been noted, nothing has been said of how 'morality' or 'moral' has been defined; as will be shown below, only Durkheim and Mueller-Deham made any serious attempt to define these terms.

2 The major focus of work by sociologists has been at the societal and institutional level.

3 Despite the interest shown at the structural level in the evolution of morals, not even the two accounts undertaken at the level of action tried to locate the seeds of change in moral codes at the interpersonal level.

4 It would seem, then, that in this context some attempt must be made to define 'moral' in sociological terms in such a way that enables an analysis to be developed which will allow a focus at the interpersonal level on the construction of moral reality in formal educational systems.

A definition

Philosophers have spent much energy in trying to define 'moral'. Thus, Hare (1952) gave a formal definition – fundamentally based on overriding prescription and universality, whereas Baier (1971) gave one based on the range of issues involved – fundamentally utilitarian in character. More directly relevant to this context is the work of John Wilson who has analysed the constituent parts of moral education. He has identified four elements, to each of which he has given a Greek-based name (J. Wilson, 1973, pp. 38–9). PHIL is concerned with understanding the concept of a person; EMP relates to having the concepts of and being able to identify with various emotions; CIG covers the mastery of the factual knowledge relevant to moral decisions; and KRAT is concerned with alertness to moral situations and the ability to make and carry out moral decisions.

In this analysis Wilson was trying to produce a universal conceptual structure for moral thinking into which content could be fitted. By its very nature moral content is value-laden and Wilson wanted to enable schools to teach their pupils to think in moral terms without prescribing any one value position. The four elements that he arrived at by *philosophical* analysis to some extent do parallel the conclusions about how teenagers make moral decisions that we shall come to as a result of *sociological* analysis in the next chapter.

Sociologists, however, have either ignored the task of defining the concept 'moral' or given it a low priority. Thus, Ossowska (1971) included in her book a brief introductory chapter on 'distinctions' in which she outlined her approach, but ultimately concluded by analogy that religion was difficult to define and that 'since the sociology of religion can boast of some achievements, it may also be possible to discuss questions of a sociology of morality without defining morality precisely' (p. 173). Durkheim gave the rather general and sweeping definition of morality as 'a totality of definite rules' (1961, p. 26) that one might expect from his somewhat authoritarian and consensual approach. Mueller-Deham, however, gave a new emphasis both to the powers of choice that the actor himself has and to the interpersonal aspect of morality, when he defined morals as 'the internal bindings which the individual imposes on himself for himself and toward those whom he is willing to respect in his dealings with others' (1944, p. 9).

In view of the conclusions of the first section of this chapter, and particularly because of the emphasis put upon the concepts of 'the interpersonal level' and 'social change', it is proposed here to define 'moral' in a way that builds on Mueller-Deham's emphasis on interaction, but also permits the possibility of examining change in moral codes. *Morality will be seen as relating to the principles concerning how we choose to act in situations where there are consequences for others*. A number of points arise from this definition:

(1) What are principles? Peters has defined a principle as 'that which makes a consideration relevant' (1974, p. 286). Formally this is a useful statement, but a sociologist must give it substance. The principles used to decide whether any consideration is relevant to a given moral choice depend upon a range of issues to

which sociologists have given much attention, namely beliefs, values and norms concerning what is worth while and also the manner in which these are learnt in childhood. This use of the word 'principle' indicates, then, that the choices with which we are concerned are governed by beliefs that are met more widely than in the singular and occasional meetings of individuals, though it is in just such meetings that changes in moral codes may sometimes be generated.

A further point must be made. There has been no attempt here to exclude those prudential choices which masquerade as morally principled choices. This category has given philosophers much trouble. Some have not considered useful virtues to be moral virtues. Durkheim himself supported this position when he said, 'an act is not moral, even when it is in substantial agreement with moral rules, if the consideration of adverse consequences has determined it' (1961, p. 30). However, the stance taken here is that, if even some of the actors involved see a choice as moral, then the sociologist must at least start by taking account of this social definition and must at least begin by examining the act concerned as if it were a moral one.

(2) On at least two counts this definition is narrower than that often given to 'morality'. Thus, since the situations with which we are concerned have consequences for others they are social. That is, a moral choice relates to other human beings. Except when there is some consequence for human beings animals are here excluded, though interestingly the Greek concept 'ἀρετη, usually translated as 'virtue', did cover behaviour towards animals.

One obvious, and usual, consequence of this emphasis upon social interaction is that all evaluation of things, as for example in aesthetics, is excluded. But so too are evaluations of oneself that do not have consequences for others. An example would be self-judgments about masturbation. Such evaluations are generally seen as moral in nature, but here must be excluded or categorized as 'ethical', a term which must then be defined more widely than 'moral'.

(3) Behaviour is the primary focus, not attitudes or thoughts, unless these result in actions. This does not, however, exclude from sociological interest such situations as those in which an attitude favouring a certain action does not lead to the action normatively prescribed in a given society. Indeed, the very way in which this last problem has been posed assumes an accepted moral principle.

(4) Since choice is central, alternatives are available. Therefore, there is the possibility of creating new moral rules. The process of constructing morality may lead to a reconstruction of the accepted moral code; it may lead to small, or to great, change. The essential point is that change can take place. Clearly this is implicit in making choice the key to the definition of 'morality'. It is, therefore, proper that there be further discussion of this focal concept.

Choice

Sociologists of education have made use of the concept of socialization in their considerations of how children become members of a society. Until very recently there has been a tendency to view this process in a very deterministic way. Children were brought up; they had little room to choose for themselves what sort of person they might become. More recently, perhaps especially since the publication of Berger and Luckmann's *The Social Construction of Reality* (1967), a new perspective has been used, clearly indicated by the more *determining* element in the title of this seminal book. Despite some criticisms, particularly of what some see as the rather loose methodologies involved in some examples of contemporary interpretative sociology, the focus now in work on socialization is much more on how, *within* structural constraints, a child constructs his world and, hence, on the way in which actors interpret their social environment. We are all seen to be agents constantly reinterpreting the world around us (Stanley, 1973, p. 419). There is, therefore, always the possibility that a child may construct an alternative version of reality from that of his elders.

Clearly in such a view of socialization the act of choice between alternative versions of the world or of different ways of behaving must be central to any analysis of how, or, indeed, of whether the world as it now exists is reconstructed or not. Apart from a paper by Schutz (1971a), upon which much of the next chapter will be built, very little has been written by sociologists about choice as a concept. The field of occupational choice forms, however, an exception. Here, and most relevant to the topic of moral choice, Haystead (1971) has used the work of Glaser and Strauss on awareness of dying to build a framework with which to analyse the choice of occupation by adolescents. Drawing from her work (pp. 83–6) we can divide the position of someone facing a moral choice into two components: the actor's definition of the situation of choice and the social structural situation of choice, including any elements of constraint on the processes involved.

The actors definition of the situation of choice

Much moral action depends upon doing in a routine manner or without much conscious thought what has been learnt as right. Where the action is not mere habit and the actor is aware that a decision must be made he usually chooses to apply the relevant principle, as will be seen from the data to be reported in the next chapter, without challenging it. However, from time to time he does just this and may well establish a new moral rule for that situation. In a somewhat wider context, but very relevantly, Stanley writes of 'the never-ending mosaic of negotiations that comprises society itself' (1973, p. 424).

In the situations where he makes no challenge the actor works routinely within the accepted commonsense ideas of right and wrong that he has learnt from his past experience, gained either when negotiating his way through similar situations or as an unquestioning and relatively powerless member, for example, of his family of origin or of a school class. From his biography to date he has developed the personal style which governs *his* judgments of his current working morality and, thereby, reinforces it or reconstructs it for use in similar future situations.

The way in which any actor defines a moral situation must, therefore, owe much to those who have helped him to construct his moral code, that is, those who have helped him in the past or influence him now in his definitions and redefinitions of what is or is not socially respectable behaviour. These 'agents of respectability' (Ball, 1972) may include amongst others parents, headteachers and such more or less permanent or temporary cultural heroes or villains as Florence Nightingale, Adolf Hitler, Superman and the Beatles, though who such agents were or are must be seen as problematic and as a subject for empirical enquiry.

The social structural situation of choice

Choices are made in situations. Indeed, the ways in which the agents of respectability themselves are structured in any society may for some purposes be seen as part of the situation. In a sense we are searching here for some objective reality against which to measure the definitions of actors. Clearly most traditional societies differ from many contemporary societies along two dimensions. The boundaries of groups are less permeable and roles are more tightly drawn – Mary Douglas (1970, pp. 102–5) has called these dimensions 'group' and 'grid'. As a result choice is presumed to be wider today than of yore. Yet, in this respect there are cultural differences between contemporary societies. Thus, in the USSR some choice is permitted, but not so much that citizens ever become autonomous, that is, reach the psychologist Kohlberg's final stage of moral development (Kohlberg, 1971); one, that as Peters has pointed out, is seen in the USSR as 'an aberration of individualistic societies' (Peters, 1974, p. 349).

The tolerance which permits wider choice in some societies than in others is clearly a crucial factor sustaining what many see as the plurality of contemporary moral systems. This plurality complicates the moral learning of the young, even though because of their youth they are seen as 'not yet persons' (Goffman, 1952) and, hence, are permitted some moral failure. In recent times the power of the young has probably been allowed to grow inasmuch as they now appear to be permitted to make moral choices for themselves sooner than used to be the case; furthermore, they are often not compelled to choose in the way that their elders, whether teachers or parents, feel that they ought to do. Choice in such a free situation may be difficult for those who are morally inexperienced.

When in the last section we were examining how the actor defined his situation we were in part beginning to answer Harding's first question: where do our values come from? Now in considering the structural situation our focus has switched to his second question: what restrains us in our moral behaviour? This is an important focus because autonomy may well bring moral change. It is neutral moral behaviour that sustains the moral status quo. Positively evaluated deviance, known variously as creativity or as saintliness, and negatively evaluated deviance, known as naughtiness when of minor importance and as delinquency when legal action ensues, can both lead to changed moralities. Durkheim, who is often seen as holding a somewhat static view of social structures could still, long before Sartre used that fashionable word, 'project', write, 'A plan of action that we ourselves outline, which depends only upon ourselves and that we can always modify is a project, not a role' (1961, p. 29). Clearly changes in moral codes do occur. Sometimes they can be traced to such individual decisions. Almost always in trying to explain

26

them it is worth while to take the structural approach, as we shall do in Chapter 4, and to see whether there have been any changes in the power structure at societal or organizational levels so that the conditions of reciprocity are altered at the interpersonal level. Yet even this type of approach overlooks that cheapest of all moral policemen, namely the conscience.

Much of the moral teaching that is given to children by parents and at school aims to have children control their own behaviour towards others in the ways that those doing the teaching, society's agents of respectability, wish it. Psychiatrists, influenced by Freud's concept of the super-ego, have given much thought to what is generally called 'conscience'. But sociologists have 'rarely examined concepts such as guilt and conscience. It is, therefore, urgently necessary to distinguish between the reflexive guilt of an autonomic nature and the guilt arising from conflict of consciously embraced values and expedient behaviour.' Taylor *et al.*, 1973, p. 52) This is a hint which will very briefly be taken up in the next chapter.

Mental health

The mention of psychiatry raises two difficult and closely related concepts that will become important in Chapter 4, namely the concept of mental health and also that of mental illness which is in some respects the obverse of mental health. These concepts are present in Durkheim's analysis, though there expressed in a functional manner: 'All life is thus a complex equilibrium whose various elements limit one another; this balance cannot be disrupted without producing unhappiness or illness.' (1961, p. 39)

Such a view when translated into practice can lead to 'a sort of socio-technics, a hygiene of social life' (Ossowska, 1971, p. 12). Thus, there are in most contemporary industrial societies social workers of various types who see their task as helping those in difficulty to fit into their environment, though some contemporary radical social workers take the opposite view, namely that the social structure should be changed so that their clients can, without themselves changing, fit into society. Social workers can have a substantial influence in childhood and adolescence, periods when self-identity is being formed in interrelationships with others. Since the nature of interpersonal relationships is the very stuff of morality, the formation of self-identity, linked as it may be to conscience, can be central to social control in any society.

Therefore, the ruling notion of mental health is a crucial part of the general view of morality.

The Durkheimian view of mental illness locates its causes in malfunctions of the social structure. A well-known version of this theory was produced by Merton (1957). He posited that a major cause of deviant behaviour, certainly in contemporary US society, lay in a disjunction between socially produced aspirations for success in life and the lack of structurally provided opportunities for its achievement. Though this explanation may in part be true it is by no means the whole story and today much more attention is given to other explanations, mainly interactionist in nature.

In these contemporary theories the questions asked are of this nature: how do persons come to be seen and labelled as deviant – or, in our context, immoral? And, again, who has the power to make such labels stick? In connection with the first type of question, particular attention is given to the situation in which the label of immorality or lack of respectability is negotiated. The second type of question raises the issue, already assuming importance here, of who it is that does society's 'respectability work' (Ball, 1972, p. 339). This situational approach raises a further and rarely considered question: how bad must any individual be to gain the label of immoral?

There is at least a case for predicting that the stigma of being seen as immoral will have more serious consequences for an individual if it relates to an aspect of behaviour which is exhibited in several social positions or in the social positions that are seen as central to self-identity in the society concerned. Thus, in our society today a rapist or a murderer will be seen as immoral *tout court* whilst a boy who cheats in class will not usually be stigmatized outside the classroom and certainly not out of his school.

All such discussions of deviance can be seen to have a key element missing. Though it is true to common experience that persons are, often without much cause, labelled as immoral in interaction yet this says nothing about where the labels of immorality that are used in the society concerned come from. Stanley has pointed out that 'there are certain things that are perceived by people in the common sense mode as morally intelligible (or not) in and of themselves, not as a result of some conscious appeal to a subjective arsenal of assessment attitudes.' (1973, p. 404) These 'intrinsic rights and wrongs are socially prescribed and historically inherited. It is for this reason that so much attention will have to be given to tracing the recent history of moral codes and to attempting to locate any changes in who society's agents of respectability are. Much of the past moral history of any society inevitably remains as a powerful influence on the present.

Given this historically oriented view of the interpersonal situations in which moral action is occurring it is nevertheless true to say that some persons are subject to structural stresses that result in behaviour – for example, persistent adolescent violence – which is not defined as immorality but as mental illness. In such cases the individual is seen as unable to lead a normal social life. Sometimes the mental illness can be attributed to a psychological cause; something is, for example, wrong with the brain or the metabolism. In these cases clearly the person concerned is not fully responsible for his actions. He is as sick as someone who is physically ill. We attribute no moral blame to a patient with tuberculosis, though, where a disease is avoidable, as is usually the case with venereal disease, in our society some people do see the sick person as immoral or at least as responsible for his illness. Mental illness, however, often cannot be attributed to a definite physiological cause. Somehow or other the sick person has come to be unable, or to refuse, to accept others' definition of reality and it is of the nature of mental illness that the self cannot be disassociated from the illness. In all cases of non-physiological mental illness it is, therefore, important to decide how responsible for his own actions the patient is. Thus, in large measure the decision to be made is whether the label to be applied is that of sick person requiring medical treatment or of immoral person in need of some form of moral education.

'What illness *is* depends on our concept of "normality"' (Wilson, 1969, p. 56). The psychotic or neurotic person can be said to display irrational behaviour according to our present standards of normality. Such standards change. What would once have been an immoral way of treating the opposite sex is now often seen as the equivalent of marriage. There are also quite wide ranges of tolerance to what is deemed to be normal, but central to the concept of normality in advanced societies is some view of what is rational behaviour. The reasonable or mentally healthy person uses concepts and language in a logical manner and relates means to ends. Such a person is accepted as responsible on one proviso, namely that his goals are seen to lie within the 'shared abstract moral meanings' (Douglas, 1970, pp. 20–6) of his society.

Mental health must not be taken for granted in any society because much 'mislearning' occurs in the upbringing of any child. His parents may be ignorant because, for example, of their own lack of experience or prejudiced because of the way in which they themselves were brought up (Wilson, 1969, pp. 46–8). For such reasons, basically rooted in their biographies, children may behave immorally towards coloured persons or foreigners. Mislearning can be corrected by moral education, but the function of the teacher in this process is not the same as that of the doctor in his work. The teacher instructs; the doctor cures. However, the aim of each is the same, namely to make the child a socially responsible person, but the methods used will be different, because the teacher sees the child as bad or naughty whilst the doctor defines his patient as mad or mentally ill. Yet, once again, the point has to be made that even this apparently medical judgment cannot be made without involving a value-judgment in deciding how great a degree of individual responsibility can be attributed to the possible patient. Furthermore, it should be remembered that in some cases those who want to change a society politically have not been defined as witches, heretics, traitors or criminals, but as mentally ill and hence as patients to be cured by medical means.

Conclusion

From an examination of past work by sociologists on the topic of morality the conclusion has been drawn that, certainly in relation to moral education, the most fruitful point to start this analysis is to examine carefully how children make moral choices. There has, however, been some tendency in the past to analyse such interpersonal situations in a vacuum by ignoring the relationship between specific behavioural settings and the wider social structure. Here the strategy to be followed will be to try first of all to extract from data gathered from children, in this case teenagers, how they make moral choices, what are their definitions of the constraints on their situations and, especially, who are their agents of respectability.

A consequence of this approach is that the problem is raised of how much the present structure of choice, contemporary values and currently operating definitions of morality depend upon the present social structure and how much on what is now history. Though a historical approach cannot lead to predictions of future states of morality it can at least help towards a fuller understanding of what now exists and give a view of some of the constraints on the future probability of change and the direction in which movement may be possible.

Although at this point we need not take sides in the everlasting battles of what is right and what is wrong, we cannot avoid the realization that judgments of value inevitably govern individual decisions about morality. Those who, as parents, teachers or social workers, take it upon themselves to influence the growth of the self-identity of others must make such decisions. Contemporary complex societies employ agents to do their respectability work who often talk in terms of mental health. Problems that sociologists tend to define neutrally in terms of modern theories of deviance are, whether consciously or not, seen judgmentally by such agents. Decisions are made about the nature of a person's behaviour. He may be seen as physiologically sick, as psychologically ill or as plain immoral, and crucial to this attribution is the degree of responsibility and rationality seen in the individual perceived as deviant. At each stage of this decision social factors are at work; what is seen to be responsible or rational differs both cross-culturally and between historical periods, and what is perceived as deviant also varies by society. The ultimate decision as to which category of deviant a person fits into governs whether he is treated as sick or bad. The parents, the teacher or the doctor all use their version of societal norms both in deciding about and in treating the individual before them. In just the same way in which scientists can be said to solve their problems by using the current paradigms of normal science applicable to their discipline, Barnes has suggested that 'people ... seeking to determine whether a person is responsible for his behaviour [can] be described as operating with social paradigms' (1969, p. 97). In some respects this book is about important aspects of the history and nature of the application of the British paradigm of morality.

3

Moral choices

All that can be done is to exhibit the passage of the moral agent through perplexity.

(McIntyre, 1971, p. 107)

This chapter contains three parts. In the first part the process whereby children make moral decisions will be analysed and in the second part the values upon which they seem to base their choices will be examined. In the third and final part something of what is known about the present views of teachers, parents, children and others concerning moral education will be set out.

In the first two parts some data gathered during 1976 from adolescents in a co-educational comprehensive (1600 pupils) school and in a direct-grant (420 pupils) school for boys will be used; both schools are in a city in south-east England. Sixteen fifteen-year-olds were interviewed. The interviews were semi-structured, lasted between seventeen and thirty-five minutes and were taped. Eleven were with pupils, six boys and five girls, from the large comprehensive school and five were with boys at the direct-grant grammar school. One of the boys and one of the girls from the comprehensive school were by request known delinquents; the remaining teenagers were chosen by their schools as average students. In addition, a sentence completion test, based in the main on that devised in the sixties by the Eppels (1966) was given to a sample (N=77) of the same age in the same two schools. In the comprehensive school boys (N=27) and girls (N=25) were involved. In both cases the test was completed anonymously under classroom conditions.

The establishing of a well-founded conceptual framework within which moral choice can be considered is an essential preliminary towards deciding how to set about teaching the moral curriculum in schools. Here the small amount of evidence gathered will be interpreted with the intention of suggesting a primitive conceptual framework that will at least open up the possibility of adding a sociological dimension to the analysis of and curricular development in moral education. Only when those responsible for such teaching, and in British primary schools this really means every teacher, know how to conceptualize moral choice can they prescribe curricula which have some chance of achieving their aims.

Moral decisions: a sociological account

Introduction

Principles are usually taken for granted and followed unconsciously 'until further notice' by the moral 'man in the street' 'who has a knowledge of recipes indicating how to bring forth in typical situations results by typical means'. But occasionally an actor will be questioned so that he has to support his actions in terms of the principles that he feels are involved. Then he will undertake a reflexive monitoring of his conduct in order to present an account that will justify what he has done in a way presumed acceptable to his questioner. The actor in some small respect moves towards becoming a morally 'well informed citizen' who neither labours under the narrowing disability of being 'possessed of expert knowledge' nor 'acquiesce(s) in the fundamental vagueness of a mere recipe knowledge or in the irrationality of his unclarified passions and sentiments' (Schutz, 1971b, p. 122). On such an occasion principles are made manifest and actors are either compelled to follow generally accepted principles or they become moral entrepreneurs responsible, perhaps in some small way, for changing the local, or even the wider, moral climate.

Most moral decisions follow in a routine way the commonsense recipes that have been learnt prior to the present. Only rarely do we, in a manner somewhat akin to Garfinkel's Agnes (Garfinkel, 1967, pp. 116–85), look back in retrospect to produce a moral explanation to justify what we have already done. Even more rarely do we meet new situations where we have to reflect on the circumstances before we can decide to act morally. In the rest of this section data drawn largely from the interviews will be deployed to give an interpretative account of, first, recipe decisions and, second, reflective moral decisions.

Recipe decisions
Towards the middle of each interview respondents were asked, 'Do you find it difficult to make decisions when you have to?' Eleven claimed to have no difficulty in this respect. They were also asked how they thought a person knows what is right and what is wrong; twelve respondents, including all the boys at the direct-grant school, answered in such terms as 'from their bringing up' (Comprehensive Boy – CB). Peers were also mentioned as a source of ideas, 'People talk about what's right and wrong all the time' (Comprehensive Girl – CG).

One boy in particular related his upbringing both to the learning of principles, rather than rules, of behaviour and also to his ongoing experience: 'I think I've been pointed in the right direction and from that I've got my ideas ... from my experience' (Direct Grant – DG).

What, then, is the nature of the main principle or principles which act as recipes for moral decisions?

Actors bring to situations where moral decisions have to be made vocabularies of motives (Gerth and Mills, 1954, pp. 112–29) that they have learnt beforehand. These vocabularies can both provide actors with responses to most questions of justification that may be asked and limit the possibilities of replies open to them. Thus, the thought may occur to the moral actor, 'If I did this what could I say?' There is much evidence both in the interviews and from the sentence completion test that the main principle underlying moral behaviour can be summed up in the question of one girl, 'Will it do any harm to anyone?' (CG).

However, moral principles are not invariable rules and these teenagers were aware of the naivety involved in the unbending following of rules. They gave some indication of their manner of trimming to circumstances in dealing with cues presented to them in their interviews which forced them to consider various situations in which lies might be told. The telling of lies was not congenial to them, but, when the lies were seen as legitimate, they were justified in terms of the overall principle already indicated of not hurting others. As one boy rather confusedly put it; 'I don't like telling lies at all ... unless you are trying to save someone from distress you feel justified more' (DG). Two other examples from other areas of moral action show a similar appeal. A refusal to steal was justified in much the same way by the delinquent boy when he said: 'I've never stolen a bike. I've thought about it when I was walking along. But ... where does that leave the other person?' (CB). Finally, in discussing decisions about family holidays a boy claimed that he did not always push his own wishes too hard because 'it could be selfish for me to just say I'm not doing that' (DG). The commonest reason given in these interviews for departing from a naive following of the principle of truthfulness related to covering up for one's friends. Respondents usually spoke of telling 'white lies', which were defined by a girl as 'when you tell lies not to hurt someone' (CG). Once again the importance of the principle of the good of others is demonstrated since it is here used to overrule the principle of truthfulness.

These learned recipes that guide moral decisions are related by some, including four of the six girls at the comprehensive school and one boy from the direct-grant school, to a notion of 'conscience'. One girl described this as 'a sense inside you' (CG). In general, conscience was seen as learnt, though one girl definitely – the others were uncertain – felt that there was an 'inborn' (CG) element. What in general discourse is spoken of as 'having scruples' was a felt experience to these teenagers. A boy said, 'It's often more difficult when you've told the lie and your conscience tells you you should go back on it' (DG). This seems to have been a case of 'guilt arising from conflict of consciously embraced values and expedient behaviour' and should be distinguished from the next example which seems to demonstrate 'reflexive guilt of an autonomic nature' (Taylor et al., 1973, p. 52). In this case a boy, speaking in more specific terms about telling lies to his mother said. 'Because my mother trusts me I feel guilty telling lies' (CB).

The application of the learnt moral code upon which a teenager at the moment is operating usually appears to be unconscious or routine. However, situations do occur from time to time which force an actor to consider how he should behave and whether he should in some way alter, even if minimally, his moral code.

Some indication of how teenagers react to these situations can be seen in the ways in which the sample completed the sentence, 'When I have more than one choice I usually ...' 26 per cent replied in terms of careful thought, 26 of considering themselves, 18 of considering others, 16 of indecision and 5 per cent, all boys from the direct-grant school, claimed to resort to chance methods (9 per cent of replies fell in the miscellaneous category). Apart from the last case there seemed to be no differences in the ways in which boys and girls answered this question.

Those events which force a reconsideration can cause the veil of routine to be torn asunder. For teenagers the commonest cause of such reconsiderations appears to be what may be called 'temptation situations'. Thus, the friends of one boy wanted him 'to steal from a grocer's shop'; he consulted his mother who 'told me to leave off with those friends', which he did 'for a time' (CB). Two boys spoke of being offered cigarettes; one refused 'because I'm a boy athlete' (CB) and the other 'ignored it' (CB). The delinquent boy gave a vivid example, though perhaps expedience was also at work in his case. He was with a friend and 'saw this bike without no padlock. My friend said, "It'll get us home quicker." I said, "You must be mad. Put it back. I'll have nothing to do with it if you get nicked" ' (CB).

In all these cases, despite the crisis, the ruling recipe remained unchanged. There were several signs that these teenagers did meet many changing situations within a relatively stable social structure. However, as they grew older, their lives became more complex and they developed new interests which automatically ensured that overlapping and competing sets of behavioural expectations faced them with decisions about what they ought to do. When commenting on the effect of upbringing in the family upon moral views one boy said: 'But you get conflicts between opinions, when you become fifteen or sixteen and your friends start to give you different views and it's up to your own choice ...' (CB).

When discussing lies respondents were given two prompts that related to age, namely, concerning going into pubs and into cinemas showing 'X' films below the legally permitted age. The general view about lying under such circumstances is summed up in this reply by one of the girls: 'Lying about your age. I don't really call that a lie. It's not really – unless they ask your age' (CG). In such circumstances one boy said he was 'prepared to weigh out a thing'. When asked whether he now just followed his parents or weighed things up, he replied, '[I'm] now a weigher-upper, but [I've] still got some of the ideas of my parents' (DG).

So far we have been considering behaviour that is either projected or capable in retrospect of interpretation as projected (Schutz, 1971a, pp. 71–2). Some of the respondents did, however, admit to what may be called impulsive behaviour. Thus, the delinquent boy hit his sister and then asked himself, 'Whew! What did I do that for?' and could find no answer in his present vocabulary of motives by which he could explain what he had done.

To this point an attempt has been made to give an account of the recipe decisions of moral 'men-in-the-street'. Teenagers believe that these recipes are largely learnt from their families, but that, as their experience widens, they are forced into situations where they have to re-examine their recipes. It is to this process of active creation, rather than re-creation, of moral codes to which we must now turn.

Reflective decisions

We are, therefore, now concerned with situations where 'the individual sees himself as being faced by competing alternatives requiring a "choice" between them' (Haystead, 1971, p. 83). He is *aware* of the need to come to some decision and is forced to behave more like a morally well-informed citizen. There is a tendency for social scientists to see this process as a highly rational procedure, comparable in its properties to the workaday decisions of an expert, usually seen in terms of a natural scientist. Garfinkel (1967, pp. 262–83) has, however, shown that commonsense activities by their very nature lack elements of clarity, of formal logic and of compatibility between means and ends. Inasmuch as everyday moral decisions are commonsense activities they must be highly uncertain and problematic in character. Yet, as Schutz has pointed out, the morally well-informed citizen does try, as far as is possible, to overcome the problems that Garfinkel indicated.

Thus, Schutz (1971a, p. 30) describes the process of commonsense choosing in this way: 'Each of the alternatives standing to choice has . . . to be rehearsed in phantasy in order to make choice and decision possible.' One boy in his interview said: 'If there are a lot of alternatives it makes it that much more difficult, but it's usually, "You do it or you don't" ' (DG).

The actual balancing between known alternatives can be conscious and the problematic aspects may be of low salience. One boy was keen both on work for the St John's Ambulance Brigade and on going to a local disco and sometimes the chance to participate in both activities clashed; he decided between the two courses according to whether or not he could 'put [the other] off till another occasion' (CB). Another boy told of a decision that was technically perhaps as simple as the last example, but that was fraught with much greater consequences, namely not to pay his fare on a bus, 'You just look out of the window and the conductor asks, "Any more fares?"' (CB).

But most moral decisions have more imponderables than the last two examples. A decision that shows a high degree of complexity is provided by the case of a boy whose parents wanted him to go to London with the family to see a play on a day when he had been invited to go to a party. Ultimately he went with his parents:

> It was partly I'd said beforehand I'd go. Partly the tickets had already been bought. It would have been a waste of money. Partly it was my mother's birthday and I'd make her happy ... I preferred Chekov's 'Seagull'. They wanted Shaw's 'Too True to be Good'. But it was mother's choice because it was her birthday. (DG)

This incident indicates three elements crucial to the analysis of moral decisions, namely: the structure of knowledge at hand to the process, e.g. knowledge of the drama; the factors considered by the actor to be relevant to that situation, e.g. the economic factors; and the actual and likely interpretations of others of the actor's possible behaviour, e.g. the mother's feelings.

Clearly there is a vast amount of sheer factual knowledge which any actor brings to each moral decision. In addition, there are his current operating recipes of right and wrong to which reference has already been made. But these resources may not be sufficient to the project on hand either in the actor's own estimation or in that of others who are concerned with his decisions. Thus, one boy in discussing making a decision said, 'You compare it with the past. It's not quite the same as the past, but you find general differences' (DG). This process of comparison isolates the principle to be applied, the degree of ignorance or knowledge and, most important of all, the goals held at the time for the project in hand.

These goals will be expressed almost inevitably in terms of learnt vocabularies of motive. There is a problem of how 'real' the expression of such motives is. The delinquent boy claimed to subscribe to the principle of telling the truth, but yet said, 'I'd lie to save my skin' (CB). There is a body of sociological theorizing that supports the psychological concept of internalization. Thus, motives which are firmly sanctioned by a surrounding close-knit network are seen as more likely to be internalized than those expressed by actors in, for example, a highly differentiated urban society, where sanctions are less easily brought to bear on persons interacting in the many loose-knit groupings present in such a social structure. In the latter case different behaviour patterns can easily be sustained by the same actor in different settings. Thus, several of the boys interviewed said that they would swear at school when with their peers, but not at home with their parents.

Schutz has written, 'We have to learn what is interpretively relevant.' He has also differentiated between 'imposed' and 'intrinsic' relevancies. The latter he defined in relation to an actor's 'paramount theme' (1970, pp. 28–43). This focus on present goals seems acceptable, but there is possibly confusion in Schutz's views about imposed relevancies. In the passage quoted these are defined in terms of 'sheer unfamiliarity', which seems to omit all reference to relevancies brought to a decision because the actor has learnt them, having had them imposed on him, usually without choice, or because he feels that he must bring them in view of possible sanctions that may be used against him. However, in a posthumous joint work when discussing 'imposed' relevancies the point is made that 'attention can be forced socially' (Schutz and Luckmann, 1974, p. 187). In our consideration of imposed relevancies here it is this latter extended meaning that will be used.

Examples of both the mentioned categories of imposed relevancies were found in the interviews. One boy at the direct-grant school was obviously in the first situation, where relevancies had been learnt without choice: 'My parents have a fairly good idea of how they want me to behave and I go along with that because it seems sensible' (DG).

But, as indicated, the acceptance of existing typifications can be due to the existence or believed existence of sanctions. There is some evidence relevant to this point from the sentence completion test; respondents were asked to complete the sentence, 'I can't always do what I want because ...' Thirty-six per cent of the sample replied in terms of the constraints of power held by others; and two-thirds of the girls mentioned their parents in this connection. In her interview one girl described how she did not like to ask permission at table to go to the toilet because she 'was frightened of offending my granny and frightened of punishment too' (CG). Sanctions can also be imposed by or felt possible from peers. As already reported one boy told how, although he thought it was wrong, he was often tempted not to pay on a bus 'especially because I'm small', but usually he was with friends and 'they'll think I'm a kid' (CB).

The position vis-à-vis parents was complicated. Several respondents in discussing the part that they themselves played in family decisions indicated that they were only allowed to participate in decisions that did not really matter or where their parents knew that their children would decide as they, the parents, wanted. Furthermore, one girl felt that she was put in a position where her parents tried to force her to make decisions alone which she herself wished them to assist her to make, for example about whether she should go out on a Saturday night.

This last example raises the problem of whose advice should be taken once a teenager has decided to undertake some project. Or, in other words, to whom should the actor turn as a possible agent of respectability? Such advice would be intrinsically relevant to many moral decisions, for example to decisions to be taken when in trouble. There is relevant evidence from the sample doing the sentence completion test who had to complete the sentence, 'When I'm in trouble ...' Forty per cent of the girls and 12 per cent of the boys claimed that they would seek help from their families. However, when asked whose advice they would seek when making more ordinary decisions all those interviewed, except for two boys at the comprehensive school and the delinquent girl who came from a broken home, claimed that they would consult their parents, though the nature of the decision to be made would govern whether they would seek the advice of their mother or their father or, indeed, someone else. One girl said that she would ask her mother about decisions concerning clothes or jobs, her boy friends about 'quite a lot', her girl friends 'sometimes' 'because they know what you're going through', her teachers 'sometimes' about school subjects and her father 'never' except about driving 'because he had the car' (CG). Yet going to one's parents for advice about a decision is not always easy, as one boy indicated; he went to his older sister for advice about matters in which he knew his parents disagreed with him, not because of the disagreement, 'but because they may get to know something I don't want them to know' (DG).

The way in which an actor interprets others and their views of him is important both in itself and in deciding on relevancies in any one decision. One boy had recognized the difficulties and the irrationalities often implicit in such interpretations: 'I always find it difficult to make decisions as to the real character of people ... It depends on what kind of mood I am in and what kind of mood the other person is in' (DG). It is relevant to note here that in the sentence completion test a small number (11 per cent) of the respondents expressed a considerable unwillingness to pre-judge people in any way; in sociological terms they were opposed to 'labelling' others too readily.

Once again, however, interpreting others and their reactions is not a straightforward process. In at least one case a moral decision was made after considerable discussion in a group that did not only take account of others' interpretations of possible behaviour, but also, given such possible interpretations, of what would be most expedient. Thus, a girl told about how a friend had a serious and permanently disabling accident to her hand on a ferry returning from France. It was difficult to decide 'how the thing had happened and who was there at the time and if it was really important', because from the beginning it was clear that a serious accident had occurred in which financial damages might be at issue. Had the chair collapsed – in which case the shipping company was to blame? Had the girl fallen over or did a boy twist her arm? 'We all stuck to the chair, but we still don't know how she really did it, but we all more or less know' (CG). The victim is receiving damages! A further point about this example is that the final decision could be deferred and reflective discussion was possible until an account had to be presented to the authorities. Several of these teenagers in discussing difficult decisions mentioned deferral as a strategy to enable them to consider more rationally what to do.

Once an actor has decided in his mind the relevant knowledge, factors and interpretation a 'weighting' (Schutz, 1971a, pp. 93–4) must be made. The complexity of such a qualitative calculation supports Garfinkel's conclusion that commonsense rationality is of a different order from scientific rationality. In commenting on the difficulty of many decisions one boy said: 'I'd just try and weigh up all the possibilities in my head and then decide which I thought was the best to do and do that' (DG). The same boy thought decisions difficult 'when I'm not in possession of all the facts that I'd like to have. But if I do know I usually find it not too difficult.' He had been faced with the choice, indirectly moral in nature, of whether to take part in the Cadet Corps or Social Service, in both of which he was very interested, and had after much discussion with parents and peers chosen the latter, because it was not 'militaristic'. In view of the comparable complexity of many moral decisions the earlier reported finding from the sentence completion test that four boys at the direct-grant school claimed to use methods of chance, for example, 'toss-of-a-coin', in making different decisions is not, perhaps, surprising.

Conclusion

In discussing reflective thinking Schutz used a distinction suggested by Husserl, between the ways of 'grasp(ing) the meaning of previous experiences'. This may be done through a logical process – 'step by step ... polythetically' or intuitively – 'in a ray – monothetically' (Schutz, 1970, pp. 80–1). We can apply this distinction to the making of decisions, comparing routine recipe decisions to monothetic processes and reflective decisions to the polythetic grasping of meaning. Schutz sees these two forms of thinking as different in kind. He gives no attention to the possibility that there is a grey area between immediate and reflective grasping. Thus, in terms of decision-making on some occasions we may, as it were, reflect in a more or less cursory manner. If this is the case the Schutzean dichotomy may, perhaps, more aptly be seen as a continuum. Evidence has been cited that may be interpreted as showing that some teenagers do tackle some moral decisions in a routine manner and others in a more reflective manner; and that these two types of decision do seem to be of a very different kind. With this dichotomy as a starting point we can build a simple framework with which we may begin to conceptualize the process of moral choice, but there does seem to be the likelihood that in practice there is a middle area of somewhat cursory decisions about which there as yet exists no theoretical thinking or empirical research.

Much moral behaviour does apparently depend upon the unthinking and routine application of recipes that are rarely formulated in express terms. The problem is grasped and almost instantaneously the decision is made. Ultimately such solutions may even become habitual responses. Every so often, however, for one, largely unpredictable, reason or another a moral actor finds himself in a novel situation where he must refer reflectively to principles. Sometimes the inner court of conscience enforces the unconscious following of the previously ruling principle; sometimes a full consideration of the known relevant factors leads again to its conscious support. But occasionally major re-definitions of a moral code can occur. One boy at the direct-grant school said: 'My parents are Roman Catholic and I've been brought up in a Roman Catholic tradition and I'm a bit apathetic about it now' (DG). For him the change had been gradual and he attributed it to the 'influence of people around me'. In general, individual moral change is not to be compared to religious conversion. Indeed, Stanley has attributed the slow, but constant changing of a moral code to 'the casuistry of everyday life' (1973, p. 411). We can see this process must have been at work for the delinquent boy who in a very heartfelt manner answered the question about knowing what was right and wrong with these words 'I've been through most of the things that are right and wrong' (CB).

Psychologists have tended to explain this process of moral growth in terms of stages of cognitive development. Such an explanation may be relevant to why changes are possible at all. However, in view of some of the data from the interviews reported here there is at least the chance that teenagers are moving into situations where they experience conflicting expectations. Such an explanation is supported by data gathered by McPhail et al. (1972); the adolescents in their sample were 'clear that they were moving into a world of independence where the traditionally respected adult sets of values and beliefs have no in-built right to respect ' (p. 35).

This process inherent in growing-up forces them to reconsider the current operating recipes that limit their present choices and that were in the main learnt when young. This reconsideration comes at the very moment when they are beginning to feel that the power over them of home and school is less complete than they had thought. In addition, it may well be the case that in constructing their present operating code of moral recipes those younger than the teenagers here considered go through similar processes. In commonsense terms this would seem possible, but until empirical work with younger children shows it to be so this must remain an open question.

These decisions concerning moral actions that are made when in doubt are crucially important in that those who decide either support or attempt to renegotiate contemporary morality. Such decisions are at the very work-face of the production and re-production of morality. They may be contrasted with the planned experiences of formal education as the main unplanned experiences by which teenagers move from being moral men-in-the-street to being morally well-informed citizens.

The vocabulary of motives

The relevancies brought to any decision include, as has been seen, certain motives, which may have been learnt – and here Schutz's 'intrinsic' relevancies based on 'paramount themes' are crucial – or 'imposed'. Our main source here for considering such motives is the data from the sentence completion test. The instrument used was based on that originally given by the Eppels to a sample of some 250 young people between fifteen and eighteen in the London area during the early sixties (E. M. and E. Eppel, 1966). The Eppels used fifteen incomplete sentences to tap five areas: personal relationships, concepts of justice, responsibility, authority and independence, and goals and aspirations. Thirteen of the same incomplete sentences were given to a small sample (N=77) of fifteen-year-olds in the two schools from which the interviewees were drawn. The first four of the areas investigated by the Eppels were tapped in the same way, but two of the three incomplete sentences relating to goals and aspirations were replaced by two new ones in an endeavour to discover how these teenagers viewed the process of moral choice; data from these items has been reported in the first part of this chapter. In this part the remaining data from the sentence completion test will be reported. In each case the incomplete sentence will be given before reporting the findings and making any comments. Rounding of percentages has resulted in some cases where totals do not equal one hundred.

Broad comparisons between the data collected by the Eppels in the early sixties and that from the study in mid-1976 will be made on the grounds that in both cases the samples consisted of teenagers living in the urban south-east of England, though it must be remembered that the recent sample is younger in age than that used by the Eppels and that their sample had in the main left school for employment. One of the main aims of this comparison was to discover whether the frameworks generated by each incomplete sentence in the Eppels' analysis were still realistic structures to use in the mid-seventies. Investigation of any changes in the whole structure of moral values was seen to be as important as that of changes within any given structure.

Personal relationships

'The older generation ...' The aim here was to allow those in the sample to express their views of the older generation. The framework for analysis developed from their data by the Eppels was in terms of the direction of the attitudes of the respondents. It was possible to use this same framework on the more recent sample except that a neutral category had to be added. Thus, 47 (Eppels 63) per cent of these teenagers felt negative or hostile towards the older generation ('... are old rat-bags, and talk too much, and they should keep their big mouths shut', CB), 29 (Eppels 25) per cent held qualified or mixed attitudes, 17 (Eppels 12) per cent were positive or sympathetic ('... can be a great advantage to young people, their knowledge is usually far greater', CG), and 8 per cent were neutral in attitude ('... are merely the younger generation at a later stage of their life', DG). Overall these young people, whether at the comprehensive or direct-grant school, were somewhat less hostile towards older people than were those in the earlier sample. The content of responses showed this clearly in that in several responses there was the specific realization that all must grow old and also a definite sympathy for physical infirmity was often expressed. There seemed to be a tendency for the views of boys and girls to be more alike in 1976 than was the case in the early sixties.

'Young people ...' Given the chance to express their views of their peers these adolescents, who were now less critical of their elders, showed themselves to be more critical of those in their own age group. The Eppels' framework also fitted in this case without change. Twenty-nine (Eppels 25) per cent showed favourable attitudes ('... are thought of as vandals and holigans [sic] we're not like that at all', CG), 17 (Eppels 23) per cent were critical ('... should be taught how to behave especially in school where there is a lot of violence', CB), 30 (Eppels 16) per cent held qualified views either way ('... are not all rude, impertinent, little vandels [sic] that people are always making out, they are only like that because everybody tells them they are', CG), and 25 (Eppels 6) per cent had views categorized as 'Miscellaneous' ('... often feel restricted by their parents', DG). There appears to be a greater willingness to express a critical view of other young people even allowing for the rise in the category of 'Miscellaneous'. The rise in this latter category seems attributable to the number of teenagers in this sample showing an interest in having a 'good time', since many commented on the lack of facilities for doing this in the city. Interestingly, the girls at the comprehensive and the boys at the direct-grant school were both more critical of peers than the boys at the comprehensive and than both sexes in the Eppels' study.

'A good friend ...' Since friendship with peers has such a high value to adolescents in our society it was seen as important to have some measure of how the sample viewed friends. As in the first two items the Eppels' framework fitted the data, though once again with the addition of a 'Miscellaneous' category, largely to cover neutral or descriptive responses. Seventy-seven (Eppels 73) per cent completed the sentence in terms of support or security ('... will help when you are in trouble', CB) and 8 (Eppels 27) in terms of reciprocity ('... is someone who will help you in trouble ... and will expect help from yourself', DG). Girls in particular answered in terms of support and security.

Concepts of justice

'It isn't fair ...' The major categories used by the Eppels could still be used. Forty-six (Eppels 71) per cent answered in terms of Personal Grievances and 54 (Eppels 29) per cent in terms of Social Injustices. However, the details within these two categories had to be changed, particularly in relation to the second one. This was due to the apparent growth in concern about interpersonal relationships ('... that people never hardly listen to other people's point of view', CG). This tendency seemed as true for boys as girls and for those at both schools.

'It's wrong to ...' This cue was a direct attempt to draw out of these teenagers their views of moral wrongs. Findings are shown in Table 3.1 which gives an indication of the categories of wrong foremost in the mind of this sample. Once again their emphasis on interpersonal, as opposed to personal, categories can be noted. The framework used was much the same as that of the Eppels, although there was the need to include a category covering 'labelling', that is, the prejudging of others in personal relationships. Except for this the overall results were much the same in both studies; this conclusion relates to comparisons both between the sexes and the two schools.

'I deserve praise ...' The intention here was to discover what

Table 3.1   Views of some teenagers on 'It's wrong to . . .' (per cents)

	Eppels' sample	Present study
Unfairness to people	26	19
Violence	24	17
Stealing and other law breaking	16	11
Disrespect for authority of elders	8	5
Premarital sexual relations	8	5
Dishonesty	6	4
Lack of integrity	5	7
Miscellaneous: drink, smoke, drugs	5	18
label others		15
other		
Total (per cents)	98	101
Total references made	250	123
Numbers in sample	200	77

teenagers see as right, but in this case in a setting of rewards rather than punishments. The Eppels' framework included the category, 'Social/Humanitarian', which did not fit the data gathered and the new framework shown in Table 3.2 was evolved.

Table 3.2   Views of some teenagers on 'I deserve praise . . .' (per cents)

	Eppels' sample			Present study			
				Direct-Grant	Compre-hensive	Compre-hensive	
	Boys	Girls	Totals	Boys	Boys	Girls	Totals
Conformity to accepted codes	58	70	64	16	4	0	7
Do actions for others	–	–		28	13	24	22
Make efforts	–	–		44	75	72	64
Expectations of praise	13	6	9	8	8	0	5
Miscellaneous	–	–	4	4	0	4	3
Total (per cents)				100	100	100	101
Numbers	93	105	198	25	24	25	74

There may be a major change here due to a growth, particularly amongst those at the comprehensive school, in the regarding of self-effort as a virtue needing reward. On the other hand, this change may merely be related to the composition of the two samples; the Eppels' respondents were largely in the work-force whereas those in the more recent sample were all still at school. It is worth noting that the new category, 'Do actions for others' covered much more specific instances ('help a senior citizen weed their garden', CB) than did that of the Eppels' 'Social/Humanitarian'. This change parallels the already noted growth in concern for the quality of interpersonal relationships.

Responsibility

'It's hard to ...' It was hoped that the answers would show where teenagers saw difficult decisions to lie. The Eppels' framework fitted except for the easily explainable need to include a category relating to school. Results from the two samples are not dissimilar except that this new category has taken the place for those at school that the category 'Social, Political, Economic Adjustment' had for a group mainly consisting of young workers. Thirty-one (Eppels 35) per cent answered in terms of 'Conduct and Values' ('... to understand older people's views especially when they differ so much from our own', CG); 36 (Eppels 33) per cent referred to 'Relationships with Others' ('... not accept orders from another person, unless they are polite', DG); 13 (Eppels 24) per cent gave instances of 'Social, Political, Economic Adjustment' ('... believe that there is a god who made the universe etc.', CB); the remainder in both cases gave answers that were categorized as 'Miscellaneous'.

'The most important thing to teach children ...' The expectation was that this cue would lead the teenagers to express their views on education, perhaps even moral education. The earlier framework was usable here. Sixty-nine (Eppels 82) per cent answered in terms of 'Codes of Behaviour' and 11 (Eppels 13) per cent in terms of 'Knowledge'. However, the Eppels also used a category which may be called 'Skills to cope with the world' and 10 (Eppels 2) per cent of the references were categorized thus; a further 10 (Eppels 2) per cent were coded 'Miscellaneous'.

The rise in the demand for 'Skills to cope with the world' is perhaps due to the fact that the more recent study covered teenagers still at school, who saw a need to be prepared for adult life. Three other comments are worth making. First, girls (29 per cent), as was the case in the Eppels' sample, stressed the need for manners more than boys (20 per cent). Second, the direct-grant boys saw less need for 'skills' than the comprehensive pupils; perhaps these skills are taken for granted by those at the more academic school. Lastly, whereas 3 per cent of the Eppels' sample, all girls, mentioned the need for religious education, not one of the more recent respondents did so.

Authority and independence

'When people give orders ...' The expression of feelings against authority were so common that a new category was added to cover these responses. Twenty-three per cent (35 per cent of the boys at the comprehensive school) of the sample fell into this group. The proportions falling into the categories of 'Obey unconditionally', 16 per cent, and 'Obey conditionally', 47 per cent, were much the same as they had been in the Eppels' study, namely 13 and 49 per cent. However, there was a fall in the two 'Disobey' categories which was attributable, particularly in the case of the pupils at the comprehensive school, to a switch to attitudes against authority. In addition, analysis of the content of the responses shows that for those who would obey conditionally the person who gives the order and the manner in which it is given are both very important factors.

'If you stand up for yourself ...' The Eppels' framework fitted here with no difficulty. Forty-seven (Eppels 63) per cent gave 'unqualified approval' to such a course, whilst 37 (Eppels 30) per cent also emphasized the difficulties involved. There was, therefore, a growth in the proportion approving an assertion of independence, but there was also a greater realization of the possible costs of such an action.

The changing moral code of teenagers

Some attempt must now be made to draw some conclusions about the existing moral code of teenagers from the data presented from both the interviews and the sentence completion test. Those in these two small samples of young people did have a realization that moral problems and temptation situations existed, more especially outside school. They used a code of values which they believed to be learned within their families. This code was focused on a rather strong belief in the importance of the individual and the need to rely on oneself; but this belief was not a purely selfish one since it was tempered by a firm view that the

49

quality of interpersonal relationships mattered greatly, that is, that individuals other than themselves were important. Because the individual matters, to stand out against others was permissible – at least up to a point. Though honesty was largely supported as a virtue falsehood was permissible to help others, to avoid hurting others, or where it supported conventionally acceptable behaviour. In other words, there is some support for the view that young people operate a morality that depends much on social circumstances. Some philosophers term such a morality 'situational'.

Though there are some differences between the views expressed by, or inferred from the two sexes what is remarkable is the similarity between the answers of boys and girls. Girls did, however, emphasize 'manners' more than boys as a basis for behaviour and appeal to 'conscience' more often as a basis for morality, though this factor was never seen in religious terms. Indeed, the rarity of mention of religion in a field where a hundred years ago it reigned supreme must be noted. Girls also gave more importance than boys to friends as support, though many of the boys also spoke in the same terms.

Inasmuch as the more recent data is comparable with that gathered in the early sixties by the Eppels, the following main points can be made about the ways in which the moral codes of teenagers seem to have changed in the last fifteen years. The individualism and the value put upon interpersonal relationships noted above appear to have become central to the moral codes of teenagers during this period. The other major change seems to be that teenagers take a much more considered view of moral problems. This conclusion may be supported by a number of the results reported here. Thus, concerns are less bound up in a utopian way with large social problems and more often directed towards the concrete in the form of immediate personal relationships. Again, teenagers are more critical of their peers, but less critical of the older generation and they still admit to heavy reliance on their parents in times of trouble. However, they are also rather more hostile towards authority – and this attitude is not logically inconsistent with their increased sympathy for their elders; yet this hostility forces them to see the difficulties caused by their wish to assert their independence at an age when they are still inexperienced. On the whole the school is seen as an agent to teach them, not in this moral field, but in the more strictly instrumental sphere. Finally, and because of the further

50

and clear demonstration of a concern for close relationships, perhaps the most telling change of all is the apparent birth of a desire not to prejudge others by 'labelling' them in one way or another.

This view that young persons are 'cooler' in their moral thinking has also been expressed by Wright and Cox (1971) in their conclusion to a study of the changes in the moral beliefs of a slightly older group, namely sixth-formers, over the seven-year period 1963–70. They concluded in these words:

> In every instance and for both sexes there has been a significant shift in judgement, and in nearly every case the shift has been away from the unequivocal condemnation of behaviour towards a more qualified, lenient and undecided position. (p. 334)

This apparent move throughout the range of adolescence to a more considered, and hence a more rational, process of making moral decisions is important for any pedagogical account of moral education which is often seen as 'centrally concerned with the development of certain types of motives, especially with what have (been) called the rational passions' (Peters, 1974, p. 295). It is, therefore, to the views about moral education of those concerned in it that we must now turn.

Views about moral education

Children have views both about moral education and about who are their agents of respectability. The Eppels reported that their respondents most frequently mentioned as those likely to approve their behaviour 'parents, neighbours, employers and friends' (1966, p. 180). Here we shall consider the views of the children themselves, parents, and since we are dealing with those still at school, we shall put teachers in the place of employers.

In completing the sentence 'I can't always do what I want because ...' 10 per cent of the sample answered in terms of youth or inexperience. The same feelings are most poignantly expressed in a poem written by a fifteen-year-old Australian schoolgirl:

Poem of the confused

Nothing is clear or certain,
We must wait till we understand

But before understanding comes
We will be asked to decide
Many times we must decide
Without certainty or clarity
And no one can help us
No one quite knows
And this is up to us and us alone.

(Fitzgerald *et al.*, 1976, p. 157)

In view of the possibility that adolescents might find difficulties in making moral decisions it is not surprising, though somewhat at odds with our own findings, that in one recent English survey 70 per cent of the respondents expected their schools to help them in the field of moral education (McPhail *et al.*, 1972, p. 24).

Many of these young persons realize that they will soon have to move into a far different world from that of their schools or homes. Thus, one study, made in Sheffield, of the move from school into the work-force reported that those due soon to start work recognized the inconsistencies between the moral code at school and that operating at work; for example, under the former to remove wood for kindling would be theft whereas this was usually not so under the latter (Carter, 1962).

In the recent past important differences between the sexes in the rates of moral development have been found. Girls have seemed to develop moral autonomy and make more complex judgments earlier than boys, at all ages. (Bull, 1969, pp. 80–8): 'It is only in the stark issues of life and death (that) boys keep anything like in step with girls in moral insight. When it comes to personal relationships – the essence of morality – they are almost lost in the distance' (p. 88). Certainly the data reported above shows a tendency for boys and girls to be more alike than formerly, possibly another result of this unisex age.

To some extent adolescents use schools as places for their social experiments. In one English study teenagers admitted that they did in fact try out behaviour and attitudes on adults, including teachers. More than 40 per cent of those interviewed wanted 'to find out what would happen if I did X' (McPhail *et al.*, 1972, p. 50). This is an important perspective because in many schools moral education is not given as a planned part of the curriculum. Thus, in 78 per cent of Scottish primary schools moral education is 'dealt with incidentally as the occasion arises' and in 26 per cent 'mainly in the context of religious education';

in Scottish secondary schools specific lessons in this subject are only given to 17 per cent of boys and 23 per cent of girls, usually taught apart (*Moral and Religious Education*, 1972, pp. 15–22).

In this Scottish report 'the majority of teenagers ... were completely dissatisfied with religious education and the way it was approached by teacher and chaplain'. They had some pungent comments to make: 'The Headie thinks he's the voice of God' and 'It's always the Bible – what about Mao's wee red book?' But not all were against it – one girl sought help to answer the question 'Society must have a purpose, surely?' However, what apparently was wanted in general was practical help to meet difficulties, especially in the area of relationships with the other sex, problems that were perceived as very real (pp. 31–5).

Rather similar evidence exists for England and Wales in the report on a large-scale survey carried out during 1966. Amongst fifteen-year-old school leavers of those taking Religious Instruction only 22 per cent of boys and 32 per cent of girls categorized the subject as 'useful'. The percentage of those saying Religious Instruction was 'interesting' were somewhat lower, namely 18 for boys and 31 for girls (Schools Council, 1968, pp. 57 and 59).

Over 80 per cent of the teachers in McPhail's study 'mentioned ... the school's responsibility to help pupils develop an evaluative framework and to get on with others', though about half of the teachers seemed to think schools were already doing all that could be expected of them (McPhail *et al.*, 1972, pp. 24–6). Expectations of what should be done in schools have changed historically. More of the religious and moral education of children has been assumed by teachers in this century. As a result there is some confusion amongst both teachers and parents about what is expected of them. Teachers, particularly older ones, have been described as seeing themselves as 'engaged in a value struggle with powerful external agencies – a struggle which they felt they were progressively losing, mainly because parents did not support them effectively' (Grace, 1972, p. 93).

Teachers in all types of English schools have been found to define their work primarily in intellectual and moral terms rather than in terms of such social objectives as helping pupils to achieve a higher social class. However, they perceive parents as being rather indifferent to moral and social training, but as emphasizing whatever will help towards social advancement. In fact, parents in general have more or less the same objectives as teachers, putting their main stress on intellectual and moral education (Musgrove and Taylor, 1969, p. 63). Such a lack of mutual under-standing does not work towards easy co-operation between school and home.

The values that teachers appear to be particularly concerned to teach the young include honesty, a respect for persons and property, and appropriate attitudes towards work. Despite the wishes of their pupils they do not put great weight on assisting the development of sexual morality (Grace, 1972, pp. 86–8). The methods recommended to inculcate moral lessons can vary by stage of schooling and by the views of the teacher involved. Thus, one recent study of primary schools found that '70 per cent of teachers feel that informal methods encourage responsibility and self-discipline, whilst opinions are almost equally divided about this in relation to formal methods' (Bennett, 1976, pp. 56–7).

Certainly primary teachers who are in constant contact with the same school class throughout almost every day in the academic year cannot avoid teaching moral qualities in the general course of their work, and regardless of any programmed periods of religious education. It would appear that very few parents exer-cise their legal right of withdrawing their children from such les-sons. Ninety-six per cent of primary and 93 per cent of secondary heads in a Scottish sample reported that none, or less than 1 per cent, of parents withdrew their children from these lessons. It also appeared that no primary teacher opted out of teaching this subject whereas 9 per cent of secondary teachers did. Likewise, whilst 14 per cent of primary teachers were against teaching reli-gious education, 53 per cent of those in secondary schools were. Those in the north and rural Scotland welcomed the oppor-tunity to teach religious education more than those elsewhere; males, married women, and mathematics or science teachers were all more opposed than others (*Moral and Religious Education*, 1972, pp. 10–28).

Parents do play a major part in the moral development of their children since many important moral lessons are learnt before children ever start formal schooling. A great deal of evidence has shown that young persons tend to follow the wishes of their parents when making decisions about situations that are oriented towards the future, but those of their peers in situations oriented to the present. A recent American study (Larson, 1972) supports the interpretation put upon the data reported above, namely that in this context the nature of the situation does have a major effect upon the type of decision made, though the values of parents and of peers were found to have the systematic, but small, influence in the direction that previous work had shown.

Despite the obvious early power and the possible later influence of parents upon their children schools do not often take them into account in planning moral education. Thus, in Scotland, more than half of the secondary heads responding did not bring parents into consultations on the moral curriculum (*Moral and Religious Education*, 1972, p. 23). In view of the differences between their own and parents' roles as perceived by teachers this lack of co-operation might be expected to lead to conflict. Indeed, one recent Australian study confirms this view. Parents were found to be unwilling to criticize the content of and methods used in the academic curriculum, because they did not see themselves as expert in this field which was defined as the province of the professionals, but they were very ready to comment upon the moral curriculum and the ways it was taught. All, it seemed, were morally expert and not only the professional teachers (Fitzgerald, *et al.*, 1976, p. 53).

An English study has shown that views concerning the part the schools should play in moral education can vary by area of residence. Thus, parents on a municipal housing estate tended to hand considerable responsibility to the school for the behavioural development of their children because they thought the teachers covered this more effectively than themselves, but in a well-to-do residential area parents put more emphasis on the home in this respect. Though this tendency was correlated with social class the most powerful connection was with locality and this seemed to indicate the strength of the confidence that the well-to-do parents had that the nature of the other pupils in the school would support the direction of their own moral teaching (Musgrove and Taylor, 1969, p. 41).

One very common view of morality was expressed by Lord Beaumont in 1976 during a debate in the House of Lords on sex education. 'Morality is indivisible. A person who has learned how to make moral judgements will make moral judgements about sex as he or she will about anything else' (Hansard, vol. 367, cols. 165–6).

The situational view of morals would make one doubt that this is a tenable position. The matter is, however, more complex, because morality is defined in varying ways by different people. The Eppels consulted a group of 135, consisting of juvenile court magistrates, probation officers and youth leaders in London.

Sixty-three per cent interpreted 'moral' in terms predominantly of a social or humanitarian nature, 22 per cent in religious terms, 7·5 per cent in rational or psychological terms and 3·5 per cent in sexual terms. The focus that a person uses in his definition will much constrain the type of moral education that he advocates. These apparently very different definitions together with the varying support for a religious focus amongst Scottish primary and secondary teachers would lead us to two conclusions. First, there must be some tendency today towards a more pluralist, rather than a unitary, view of what morality is; second, in view of the fact that those in schools see the teaching of morality as part of their professional task and that parents may also very well see themselves as moral experts, conflict between home and school over the moral curriculum is more than likely.

Conclusion

The object of much contemporary moral education in so-called free countries is to make moral men-in-the-street into morally well-informed citizens, but to some extent, and even in non-democratic societies, the process of growing to adulthood inevitably poses questions that force many people to reconsider the moral recipes learned in childhood and routinely applied up to that moment. Reflection may follow and this can strengthen the acceptance of the applicable moral principle upon which the actor is working, or force him to decide upon a new principle. In doing both the latter alternatives a complex weighting process is carried out. To this is brought a background of knowledge and a structure of relevant issues – either brought voluntarily because intrinsic to the project on hand or imposed by others – and, finally, the skills of interpreting the others with whom the actor is involved. It is to a conceptual framework of this nature with these elements and to their weighting that moral educators must give attention.

In passing it is again worth noting that there is some similarity between these sociologically derived conclusions and those, reached by very different techniques, of the philosopher, John Wilson (1973), already outlined (p. 11) in the last chapter. The background of knowledge and the relevance structures brought to any moral decision parallel his GIG; the skills of interpreting others has something in common with Wilson's EMP; what has here been called 'weighting' is clearly part of his KRAT. Wilson also identified a fourth quality, PHIL, concerned with the understanding of the concept of a person and this may be subsumed under the sociological concept of the vocabulary of motives. But it should be noted that Wilson views this category in the same way as the other three as value-free and applicable to moral decisions in all cultures, whereas the sociological concept allows values to enter into the very structure of the decisions that are made. Indeed, there is the possibility that in the limiting cases of some cultures individuals might no longer be treated as persons. Reference will again be made in the last chapter to such extreme positions, very different as they are to what we have found to be the values apparently held by teenagers in Britain today.

Intrinsic to all projects are motives, and we must know the vocabulary of motives held by those making, or being taught to make, moral choices. Indeed a part of moral education usually is the teaching of the vocabulary of motives that is acceptable to the school concerned. Evidence presented here supports the view that teenagers tend to put at the centre of their vocabulary of motives the importance of themselves and others as individuals and the sanctity of the individual in interpersonal relationships. But they do trim their moral code to meet certain exigencies in some situations. How representative the data reported here about teenagers is of younger persons is a matter for research, but at least there is an *a priori* case for supposing such children to choose in much the same way and to have begun to learn the foundations of the vocabulary of motives that they will later hold in their teens.

Young people appear rather hostile to present attempts to educate them through formal lessons in moral education, especially when this is associated with religion, despite the fact that they do also seem to want to be helped by schools in this area of their lives. Such a paradox raises the validity of present methods and of the part played by teachers in this area of the curriculum. Teachers themselves see the moral development of their pupils as important, but in many cases, particularly in urban secondary schools, are not keen to be involved in the formal part of moral education. Yet only with much difficulty and self-control can they avoid taking some part in the informal moral education of their pupils. Parents, especially perhaps those who live on municipal housing estates and go out to work daily, have come to hand more of their former function of moral education to the school, but may nevertheless still see themselves as morally expert enough to criticize the professional activities of teachers in this field.

There are a number of important historical questions that can be raised about these conclusions. How has moral education come to be seen as so important – perhaps of growing importance – in British schools? Why have the vocabularies of motives that teenagers hold developed in this increasingly individualistic, and hence perhaps pluralistic, direction? Answers to these problems should help to explain the past and indicate some of the constraints upon the plans that can be made in the present for the future of moral education. It is to such historical questions that we shall now turn, though we must constantly remember that what we are examining is the developing social structure within which moral choices were made.

4

Changing views of morality

> To set the cause above reason,
> To love the game beyond the prize,
> To honour while you strike him down,
> The foe that comes with fearless eye,
> To count the life of battle good,
> And dear the land that gave you birth,
> And dearer yet the brotherhood
> That binds the brave of all the earth.
> (Sir Henry Newbolt, 'Rugby Chapel', 1912)

Around 1900

The verse at the head of this chapter is redolent of the morality of the English public schools in the first twenty or so years of this century. It shows clearly the connections between an approved morality and patriotism, war and games. Furthermore, the title of the poem links its moral prescriptions to Christianity as exemplified in the schools patronized by the upper middle classes. Merely to read these lines today is to be reminded that 'vocabularies of motives have histories, as their various institutional contexts undergo historical change' (Gerth and Mills, 1954, p. 118). One such context is that of social class, though we must remember that not only may contexts be different for the various classes in any country at one time, but changes may affect each class differently through time. It is to such historical processes that attention will be given in this chapter in view of the widely acknowledged importance of the relationships between social class and schooling in Britain over the last century.

The vocabularies of motive of each social class can be different, but any ruling class will be eager to assure its position by controlling what it sees as dangerous tendencies in the morality of the ruled. McIntyre (1967b, pp. 38–43) has succinctly outlined the morality of the social classes in England at the end of the nineteenth century. He sees the upper middle class as ruled by 'the morality of the public school prefect'. This code was characterized by 'loyalty to the group' which was 'the bearer of the essential past' and by 'a corresponding feeling that there are no limits to what you may do to outsiders'; in addition, members of the group had 'a right to a certain sort of job', namely as a member of the ruling class in one capacity or another. Next, the morality of the middle class was that of the businessman, characterized by 'thrift and ... hard work ... seen as a virtue in itself and not merely as a means to an end, and self-help and self-advancement (were thought to) have a maximal value ... The key relationship (was) not to the past but to the future.' Finally, the working class in McIntyre's view was characterized by a 'trade union morality' that rested on the assumption that 'a man's links are chiefly with those with whom he works'. A member of this class defined himself as 'essentially equal with those who claim superiority to him' and this knowledge was 'his chief weapon' against the other classes; his commitment was neither wholly to the present nor to the future, but he oscillated between them.

Religion, and especially in its moral context, was important to each social class. The upper middle class may not have held a fervent belief in God, but they did think it fitting to attend at and to support the established Anglican Church; some of the middle class were strongly nonconformist as were elements of the urban working class, amongst whom were also found most of Britain's Roman Catholics. Religion was very important for education, because its teaching was assumed under the 1870 Education Act which established the elementary system and under the 1902 Act through which state-financed secondary schools and training colleges for teachers became a possibility.

The provided schools were expected to teach an agreed syllabus, assumed to be Christian in character, and the state also supported a large number of denominational, particularly Anglican, elementary schools.

At the turn of the century there was still no doubt that the upper middle and middle classes ran the country. It was their view of what was respectable, even if they did not always live up to it themselves, that governed the code of morality that they wished to transmit through the educational system. It would, therefore, be amongst those members of these classes associated with schools that we might expect to find the ruling agents of respectability. If we examine, for example, those sponsoring and connected with the conference that produced the two important volumes of *Moral Instruction and Training in School* during 1906/7 (Sadler, 1908) we find that they include members of the aristocracy, of the upper middle class, of the clergy of all ranks and of several denominations, headmasters and teachers – disproportionately drawn from the public rather than from the state schools, a few politicians and one or two academics from the universities who were interested in the moral, as well as the academic, curriculum.

It is worth noting at this point that medical men were not to the fore in this conference though early in the nineteenth century they had been forced to fight to retain control of the treatment of the insane, that is, for the control of the then existing machinery of mental health (Scull, 1975). Likewise, in France doctors had gained a large measure of control over the early moral training of the working class (Boltanski, 1969). There were, however, signs that a claim by medical men to be involved in the control of morality might soon be made in Britain (Musgrave, 1977c). The nineteenth-century public health movement was dominated by medical men or men who used medical models of thought. Many public schools now had appointed medical officers. Probably the most famous of these, Clement Dukes, medical officer at Rugby, had in 1883 written *Health at School considered in its Mental, Moral and Phsyical Aspects*, the fourth edition of which was published in 1905, and the title of which clearly indicates the moral claims of a leading medical practitioner in this field.

The turn of the century also saw Britain involved, and without much initial success, in the Boer war. This failure led to much questioning of the academic and moral curricula then taught to both leaders and followers. For example, in 1900 Dr

Warre, headmaster of Eton, unsuccessfully urged parliament to force six months of compulsory military service on all secondary schools. It is to the way in which moral codes developed from this position at the start of the century until about 1960 that we shall now turn our attention.

Respectability 1900–60

The public schools
It has been said that imperialism, militarism and athleticism were during 1870–1900 the 'secular trinity' of the upper middle-class school (Mangan, 1975, p. 324). Certainly the qualities of service, loyalty and reverence to authority, already mentioned, were central both to this trinity and to the way in which the public schools were organized. Prefect systems, compulsory corps and games were all essential to the moral curriculum of these schools, indeed probably were at their strongest in the years between the Boer War and the 1914–18 war. Furthermore, despite early misgivings, particularly concerning competition and prizes, by Miss Beale, headmistress of Cheltenham College and one of the great pioneers of secondary education for girls in England, public schools for girls came to resemble 'the boys' schools not only in their emphasis on organized games but also in their curriculum, with its stress on classics and science' (Kamm, 1965, p. 220).

These same qualities remained the nub of the moral curriculum of the schools until about 1960 although the methods of teaching them changed somewhat. In his extremely well-regarded work, *The English Tradition in Education*, published in 1929, Sir Cyril Norwood, a former headmaster of Harrow, saw the main assets of this tradition to be a Christian spirit, self-restraint, English culture, the true spirit of athletics and the spirit of service (1929, p. 307). Thirty years later a Committee of the Incorporated Association of Preparatory Schools in its report, *A Reconsideration of the Aims of Teaching in Preparatory Schools* – and it may be that this category of school exhibits more extremely these values than the schools for which they are preparing – could say: '... as social creatures, boys have first to learn that the individual is less important than the whole. They have to learn to work hard at tasks which must prove uncongenial. They must be taught to develop their own abilities in order to use them for the good of others'. (Weinberg, 1967, p. 98) Manliness, then, was seen in moral terms and the public schools concentrated in their teaching of it upon an ideal often caricatured in terms of 'the stiff upper lip'. When in a supposedly medical work Dukes was discussing 'strength of character' he could write that 'it is scarcely possible to exaggerate the beneficial effect of the Morning Cold Bath ...' (Dukes, 1905, p. 39). However, extremes in behaviour of any sort were to be discouraged. In a speech day address in 1935 at the direct-grant school whose pupils formed part of the sample in the last chapter the speaker in addressing non-prize winners could say: 'There is not the slightest doubt that the back-bone of England, the backbone of the Empire, has been the moderate man' (*The School Magazine*, vol 31, p. 23).

The stress on ordinariness may in part stem from the work of Thring, the late-nineteenth century head of Uppingham, who was the first in such schools to assert and to practise the 'fundamental thesis, that every boy, not excluding the stupid, deserved individual special treatment' (Mack, 1941, p. 84). However, this emphasis on the individual, important as it was, in no way parallels the same emphasis reported in the last chapter, because in the public schools of this period the individual, as the quotations already cited indicate, was seen as having to yield much to the demands of the society of which he was to become a member.

Yet, despite this emphasis on ordinariness, prizes and competition, as Miss Beale had noted, had an important place in the organization of these schools. In 1904 at the prize day of the direct-grant school the speaker, the Master of the Rolls, could say: 'Still prizes were a wholesome, useful and successful incentive to work, inducing youths to face the self-denial and the discipline which was essential not only to winning but even to striving for the prizes.'

Competition was, therefore, built into relationships in the classroom as well as on the games field. This element of school organization was dedicated to achieving many of the same qualities as the other parts of the moral curriculum. Few schools did not have prize days and by the period after 1945 it was not uncommon for prizes to be given for moral achievements, for example, 'for being a good leader' or 'for achievement other than academic'. The paradoxical tension that such competition encouraged between the winner or the outstanding pupil and the rest or the ordinary pupils was easily subsumed under the moral teaching concerning loyalty to the leader and deference within a hierarchy.

It was their moral, rather than their academic curriculum for which these schools became famous. The desired qualities were consciously taught mainly outside formal lessons. In school chapel they were joined to the power of an old and powerful religious tradition; more particularly, the pupils' future role as leaders at home and in the Empire was set in the spirit of Christian sacrifice. On the games field, the vocabulary of motives, hinted at in Newbolt's poem, was learnt. This was concerned, for example, with playing the game, obeying the rules, and taking punishment like a man, a set of sentiments and words which permeated much upper middle-class discourse throughout life in home, at work and prayer. In his book, *Health at School* (1905), Dukes identified some of these qualities in his discussion of the advantages of school games, which, he thought

> tend to produce a well balanced mind and character ... quick response to calls of duty ... good temper ... love of justice and fair play; self-reliance; endurance; confidence in comrades; desire to excel, which ultimately becomes a noble ambition; quick judgment; aptness to act with others for the good of all; courage ... self-control ... (and a) check on morbid desires and sensations. (p. 336)

Another indicator of the moral qualities considered to be desirable is the content of obituaries of staff members that are found in school magazines. In reading these during this period one constantly comes across references to 'service' – 'more than was necessary was given', 'tolerance', 'sympathy', 'integrity'; on all these moral qualities more emphasis is put than on the much less frequent mentions of 'scholarship'.

Bamford has written of a 'subtle but organized drive by authority to sublimate the boys' self to a team' (1967, p. 83) which was at its height during the period from about 1910 to 1930. Certainly, the emphasis was strong then. A very similar emphasis was found in the public schools for girls. However, it is also true that criticisms of these tendencies began to be more common during this same period. One obvious index of this was the growth of private progressive schools, usually co-educational, non-competitive in spirit, and almost always laying great stress on individual spontaneity and growth rather than on the preparation of the individual for a particular niche in society. Mack has pointed out that for the first time in English history 'a not inconsiderable body' – he estimates 10 per cent – of parents who normally

would have sent their children to public schools found themselves in disagreement with the ideals of these schools and the
whole of their educational tradition. As a consequence they gave
their patronage to the new 'progressive' schools that were often
totally independent of the older tradition and nearly always
totally opposed to it (1941, pp. 377–9).

One index of the rise and the direction of such criticism can
be found in the changes in the nature of school stories during these
years. There was a strong tradition of stories about public schools
stemming from Thomas Hughes *Tom Brown's Schooldays* (1857)
through Dean F. W. Farrar's *Eric* (1858) to H. A. Vachell's *The
Hill* (1905). Basically these were *stories* largely for boys, though
there were some written for girls, showing how the morally good
won in the end. After 1910 school *novels* began to appear that
were aimed at adult readers. Hugh Walpole's novel *Mr Perrin
and Mr Traill* (1911), is an interesting case, since it was about
masters as much as boys, showing the adverse moral effect of a
poor school, especially upon the former group.

In 1913 Lunn wrote *The Harrovians* which in view of its style
may be categorized as a school story rather than as a school novel.
Yet it was critical of a very famous public school. Lunn condemned many of those parts of the moral curriculum seen by
heads and others as central. He was especially fierce over the spirit
of athleticism and the pharasaic nature of school religion, but he
also criticized the low standard of academic work and the pre-
valence of cribbing. In this same year Compton Mackenzie published the first volume of *Sinister Street*, a large-scale novel. This
part was about the education of its hero Michael Fane, both at
St Paul's and at Oxford. Although it was initially banned by the
circulating libraries because of its description of certain sexual
escapades, it was not openly critical of the school or the education
it provided. However, it is important in that it was a novel for
adults about boys at a public school.

During the first years of the 1914–18 war the public schools
were praised for producing the young subalterns who in a spirit of
patriotic service were keen to go to almost certain death or wound-
ing in France. But by 1916, as the war dragged on, criticisms began to be heard of the quality of the nation's leaders, who at that
time were inevitably, in view of the scant provision of state
secondary schools, largely drawn from the public schools. In
1917 Alec Waugh, an eighteen-year-old subaltern, published
an autobiographical novel about his school days at Sherborne.

This book became something of a *cause célèbre*. In *The Loom of Youth* Waugh criticized many of the same things as Lunn had done four years earlier, but did so with greater literary skill and at a time when people were more ready to listen. He did, in addition, certainly in the minds of readers at that time, make much of the homosexuality practised in some houses of some schools. It was Waugh's deep concern with the moral climate of the schools which caused public concern.

These critics were not revolutionaries. They did not wish to do away with the public schools. Their remedies were comparatively minor. Earlier leaving and the open discussion of sexual matters were advocated by Waugh. Indeed the whole discussion in the weeklies at the time of the publication of Waugh's novel was carried on without reference to the new state grammar schools despite the fact that on more than one occasion the journal concerned also carried an article about the bill that was to become the 1918 Education Act and that related specifically to the state system (Musgrave, forthcoming).

Throughout this period the new state-provided grammar schools were growing in number and in size. They were established both for boys and for girls; some were co-educational. They were administered largely by men who had been to public schools, or to other private schools that aspired to such status, and hence subscribed to the code of morality associated with the upper middle-class. Where women were involved, despite some concern shown by the Board of Education in 1913, they were also supporters of a rather similar code since the movement for emancipation of women at that time firmly held to the view that what was good enough for men would do equally for women (Kamm, 1965, p. 237). However, since these new secondary day schools largely catered for the middle class, there was a strong family influence on the pupils and this worked towards supporting a more instrumental version of the public school code, one that was more attuned to the assertive social aspirations of this social class.

However, the new grammar schools used similar means to the public schools to teach the moral curriculum. We have little evidence, literary or other, from which to judge the moral climate of the grammar schools at this time. The account in Henry Williamson's *Dandelion Days* (1930) of a small county grammar school does, however, support the interpretation given here that the moral curriculum found in the public schools was closely imitated. To see how the Board of Education interpreted this code of morality we may best turn to the views expressed officially and otherwise concerning the moral curriculum considered apt for the elementary schools.

The elementary schools

Those who ran these free tax-maintained schools were either products of the upper middle-class schools or, as was often the case of the teachers, were aspiring to a higher social class than that of their parents. It is, therefore, not surprising that the code of morality that those responsible for these schools recommended had much in common with that so far described. The hold of the public schools on British social and moral education was very strong and the outward signs of this were the adoption of school caps with badges, school mottoes, the use of prefects, prize days and compulsory games. The problems of teaching public school morality in any form were much greater in the elementary schools because they recruited a less homogeneous group of pupils, to many of whom this moral code was foreign.

When Robert Morant became the permanent secretary of the Board of Education in 1902 he began a major overhaul of the state system. One of his reforms was to issue in 1905 a *Handbook of Suggestions for the Consideration of Teachers and others Concerned in the Work of the Public Elementary Schools*. In various forms this *Handbook* was one of the main ways in which the Board tried to influence what happened in the classroom until 1945 when the elementary schools were abolished. Throughout the period and despite revisions the *Handbook* always contained a section on 'The Formation' (1905) or 'The Training' (1918) of 'Character'. The earliest version clearly shows the influence of the public school code of morality to be at work. Thus, one of the main aims of Elementary Education '... the good moral training which a school should give cannot be left to chance' (p. 8). 'History, literature and games can be used to teach moral lessons' (pp. 9–10); from the latter can come 'the creation of esprit de corps, and readiness to endure fatigue, to submit to discipline, and to subordinate one's powers and wishes to a common end' (p. 76). Teachers should 'prevent scholars from forming bad habits, and should train them in good habits' and in this context

the everyday incidents of school life will enable the teachers to impress upon the scholars the importance of punctuality, of good manners and language, of cleanliness and neatness, of cheerful obedience to duty, of consideration and respect for others, and of honour and truthfulness in word and act. (p. 9)

There is a subtle difference in tone here from writings about the teaching of moral qualities to those in public schools who were to inherit or to occupy positions as leaders. Here the moral curriculum is for the led. Sometimes this can be very clearly seen as in the following quotation in a discussion of Health Education from the Report for 1927 of the Chief Medical Officer of the Board of Education. This quotation also indicates that different moral qualities were to be taught to boys and to girls:

The girls must learn the Foundations of Motherhood; the boys must acquire the strength and skill for manual labour and understanding of the spirit and methods of cooperation. They will acquire some of this by physical training, games and team work ... (p. 83)

One doubts whether those in power saw this 'cooperation' as relating to what McIntyre called the 'trade union morality' of the working class.

The attitudes and actions of teachers were crucial to the success of this attempt to teach a version of upper-class morality to the working class. Tropp (1957) has shown how, especially in the church schools, the 'goodness' of the teacher was more important to those employing him or her than any academic qualities. Those in charge of one of the major training colleges, St Mark and St John, saw as a main aim 'on the one hand to raise the students morally and intellectually to a certain standard, while on the other we train them to lowly service ...', and in selecting candidates for entry moral qualities were ranked before those of the intellect (Gosden, 1969, p. 188). Once again there is the emphasis on ensuring the transmission of a particular version of the accepted order of respectability through a deferential corps of 'teachers', rarely in the elementary schools called 'masters', to a subservient working class.

We need to have some gauge of what these teachers did in their classrooms. One source of such information is the punishment book each school was required by the Elementary Code to keep. All punishments were supposedly entered here. A study has been made of the punishment books of thirty-four schools in West Yorkshire, Essex and Cambridgeshire over the period 1900–39

(Musgrave, 1977a). In general, the evidence supports the view that teachers did punish children, including infants, for offences against the moral qualities mentioned in the long quotation cited above (pp. 67–8) from the *Handbook*. They did so much more often in the case of boys than girls – only 9·1 per cent of all recordings related to girls. It should also be noted that the incidence of punishment did appear to fall throughout the period concerned.

This latter finding probably in part reflects the changing spirit amongst teachers as the doctrines of progressive education spread from the training colleges to the elementary schools. Rewards came to have more emphasis put upon them than punishments and more attention was given to developing the individual than to his fitting easily into society (Selleck, 1972). Though this spirit was growing more influential in the colleges before the Second World War it really did not take a strong hold in the schools until after 1945. From this basis the primary schools, founded by the 1944 Education Act, grew. Yet the ethos of an imposed and deferential morality was deeply engrained in the minds of many teachers and to a great extent survived into the years immediately following the war despite the slowly growing influence of progressivism.

The agents of respectability

Those in power had come to see the schools as a crucial agent in the transmission of their version of morality. This must not necessarily be seen as some sinister plot by the upper middle class, but largely as an extension into action of their own ideology. Teachers acted, largely unquestioned, in place of many working-class parents, and schoolmasters were in effect paid to act on behalf of most upper middle and middle-class parents. Heads did set the tone of schools in Britain and in most secondary schools chose their own staff. Hence, the appointment of a head was an important link in the whole process. In public schools this was usually done by governors, inevitably drawn from the upper middle class, or in state schools by or under the influence of permanent officials who held attitudes very much the same as those of the governors of public schools. Furthermore, the pool of recruits to these key posts were either drawn from the upper classes and 'educated' in the universities or were 'trained' in colleges after careful selection to ensure that the approved moral qualities were held. The moral curriculum recommended by the Board was controlled by those who held the same views, largely because of their own education. However, earlier in this chapter a report of the Chief Medical Officer of the Board of Education was cited and a brief account of the growth in power of members of the medical profession as important agents of respectability in the field of state education must be added here (Musgrave, 1977c).

The work of Dukes in the field of school health has already been noted. At the same time there had been a development of the view that child-rearing was an important field in which doctors could give technical advice. Yet often the prescription of good practice contained moral content. Such was the case with much that those responsible for the School Medical Service, founded in 1907, advised in respect of both infant care and of health education, then known by the apparently more neutral and technical name of hygiene. In both cases there was a constant concern with teaching 'good habits'. A relevant journal, *Health and Empire*, was begun in 1926, with the aims of maintaining the family, 'the reduction of promiscuous incontinence', and 'the elimination of those infectious diseases which such promiscuity brings usually in its train' (*Health and Empire*, 1926, *1(1)*, pp. 13–14). In 1942 the name was changed to *Health Education Journal*. The medical men were claiming a wider field as moral agents.

There had been a constant struggle from the very founding of the School Medical Service over how much power the doctors should hold in the Board (Gilbert, 1966, pp. 102–58). Initally, they were powerful enough to have control of physical training as well as hygiene. However, in the reorganization attendant upon the 1944 Education Act, despite a change of name to the more broadly sounding School Health Service, they lost control over the former field. Yet they were probably more powerful because of other contemporary developments. There was an immense growth of ancilliary staff who were either in their control or worked with medical models of thought, the majority of whom, as will be seen, were concerned with problems of mental health.

In the 1955 *Report of the Committee on Maladjusted Children* (the Underwood Committee) a list was given of all the agents concerned with the prevention of maladjustment amongst children, that is, of agents of respectability. This list had five main categories: parents; the health services, including doctors, health visitors and school nurses; the schools; the Child Guidance Service; and other agencies, e.g. clubs, the media and the marriage guidance council (pp. 132–43). Four years earlier one writer had gone as far as suggesting that 'the Home Help is the latest addition to the ambassadors of health provided by a Local Authority' (Humphreys, 1951). In at least three of the categories named by the Underwood Committee the medical men held control, and even in relation to schools and to parents their influence was great.

One important point to note is that such agents as health visitors and home helps, like the family doctor, deliver the moral curriculum into the home. Certainly, health visitors were seen officially, saw themselves and were trained to see themselves primarily as agents of health education; one of their crucial moral categories was that of the family and their main aim can be seen as the enforcement of 'normal family life'; 'normal' was, of course, defined in contemporary cultural terms (Dingwall, 1977). Such paramedical experts hold credentials vouching for their proficiency in technical fields, but their training and their practice extended their power into the field of morality, largely through the ways in which they interpreted the phrase 'good habits'.

The changing social structure

It is not too much to say that in the first decade of the twentieth century the provision of education by the state was still seen as a minimal service that taught the three Rs, Godless Christianity and deference to the powers that be. In addition, those services now falling within our present definition of the Welfare State were sketchy in the extreme and still governed by the nineteenth-century Poor Law, which was originally based on the belief that the recipients of help were morally reprehensible. The creation of the School Medical Service and the start of the provision of school meals were two of the early administrative breaks with this position. Certainly, as operated by Morant and George Newman, the Chief Medical Officer of the Board from 1907–36, this Service provided medical services as of right to all children in state schools. The administrative machinery of the Poor Law was, however, only slowly destroyed. In 1919 a Ministry of Health was established; Newman now became joint Chief Medical Officer of the Ministry and of the Board. It was not until 1929 that the Local Government Act finally eliminated the last vestiges of the Poor Law, for example, doing away with the long hated and Dickensian-sounding Boards of Guardians. What brought about these major changes, slow as they may have been in their coming?

In the late nineteenth century the power of the trade unions had grown and, as a result of the 1905 parliamentary elections, for the first time a substantial number of Labour members were returned to the House of Commons; prior to this date such members had normally sat with the Liberal Party. There was, therefore, in parliament the more powerful advocate of the working class for which the trade unions had been fighting with growing effect for some fifty years. Above all it was to the appalling poverty of many of their class that such political groups increasingly gave their attention. The work of such social scientists as Charles Booth in the 1890s and Seebohm Rowntree in the 1900s gave added legitimacy to these claims. The shocks to complacency resulting from Britain's initial defeats in the Boer War were felt by a people who still saw themselves as a great power, but they also strengthened the claims of the representatives of the working class that something might be wrong with the way in which the majority of the population were raised, housed and tended – or rather not tended – medically.

What Gilbert (1966, p. 13) has called 'the new philanthropy' was born. The belief became more common that the ills of industrial capitalism were not necessarily attributable to moral failure, but might often be the more or less inevitable consequences of economic change. In the period up to the General Strike of 1926 some modest advances were made in the provision of social services (Kincaid, 1973, p. 240), but the political consequences of that strike were reactionary and, in addition, the effect of the severe economic depression of the early-thirties was that welfare provisions were cut back rather than increased.

The Second World War drove many to a further reconsideration of the nature of the social structure for two main reasons. First, the situation of full employment that was born then, but which outlasted the end of the war, gave the working class greater power. But, second, the gap between the material and the behavioural standards of the middle and certainly the lower part of the working class was once again thrown into full light in 1939 during the evacuation of the cities which was undertaken as a precaution against possible heavy bombing by the Germans in the early days of the war. Some of the resulting feelings helped to hasten the planning for the reform of the educational system that led to the Education Act of 1944. In a period when there was some tendency for the whole country to feel unified in the face of a possible German invasion some considered that the existence of schools catering largely for the upper middle class was a divisive influence, the cause of which should be abolished.

This was not to be. Yet what was happening was that the old positions of power were no longer taken for granted. The social structure that existed in 1900 and that had been inherited from the long years of deference need no longer be accepted, not only because of its apparent inefficiency in economic terms, but, and more important, because it was now seen by an increasing number in all social classes to be unfair. In the early nineteenth century before the full impact of the industrial revolution and before the introduction of male suffrage by ballot there were many reasons why the attempt to pass on a more or less common code of morality from generation to generation could be made and why deviance amongst the lower classes could easily be controlled by those with power, whether these were landed gentry in the country or small employers in the towns. But a century later in large cities the power of many agents of respectability was less immediate in its influence and such countervailing forces as trade unions and the Labour Party meant that other views could be more easily upheld. The old definitions of morality were now seen for what they were, that is, man-made and not necessarily applicable to the whole community. Furthermore, since they were man-made, the claim that religion, particularly that of the established Anglican Church supported by the upper middle class, could be invoked to justify one particular code of morality, largely associated with the ruling class, was felt to be false (McIntyre, 1967b, p. 14). Not only had a plurality of moral codes become a possibility, but the legitimacy of the former unitary code had been upset.

McIntyre has distinguished between 'secondary virtues' such as fair play and tolerance, and 'primary virtues ... which are directly related to the goals which men pursue as the ends of their life' (p. 24). Secondary virtues relate to means, primary virtues to ends. McIntyre holds that the main elements of respectability in Britain have related to secondary virtues that 'arose out of the necessity of class compromise' (p. 35). A case can be made that by 1939, if not earlier, the agreement over secondary virtues had disappeared in the growing bitterness of class-bound politics. The agreement about such primary virtues as equal respect for all as human beings is perhaps rarely broken in most societies, though social crisis or revolutionary politics might even bring this about. In the interwar years there was some talk along such lines, but the Second World War and the struggle for national survival ended it. Yet the point to be made is that political developments had broken a very important element in the moral consensus. No longer was the working class willing to accept unquestioningly the moral code that had originated in the upper middle class and with which the public schools in particular and schools in general were associated.

The return of the first majority Labour government in 1945 made a switch in political direction possible, but it was made more probable by economic tendencies that had occurred during the war and that continued to operate in the post-war period. First, there was an increase in per capita income in real, not merely monetary, terms. This made the provision of welfare services easier and widened the scope for economic manoeuvre so that more attention could be given to measures aimed at individuals, for example psychiatric services, at the expense of bulk services, for example the total cover gained by compulsory school medical inspections. Second, the increase in real income was proportionately greater for young workers than for adults. Inevitably the options open to adolescents in work became greater. They had more chance to choose patterns of behaviour that differed from those experienced by the older generation. Whether or not there was a 'youth problem' before 1939 is not at issue, but what is important is to note that its nature was totally different after 1950. It was no longer a question of enforcing an agreed code of morality, but rather of deciding which acts were allowable and which were not, amongst many possible available ways of behaviour in relation to dress, interpersonal relationships, and orientations to the future, to the family or to the nation.

Such decisions became more important in the late fifties because of changes in the demographic structure. Following the war there was a 'baby boom' so that the number of adolescents was inevitably greater by 1960. Furthermore, the changes that affected young people at work had implications for the increasing number of those of the same age now remaining in secondary education. Thus, moral changes were bound to affect the schools, certainly at the secondary level.

An additional tendency at work was that greater wealth was accompanied by a changing pattern of disease. Rickets and tuberculosis almost disappeared whilst obesity, dental caries and behavioural problems grew more common (*The School Health Service*, 1976). Above all there were now available the resources to meet the apparent need to treat an increasing number of both adults and children who were suffering from some form of mental illness. The tendency for more children to stay on longer at school meant that the schools were more often involved with such cases. In addition, there was a rise in juvenile delinquency and to take any measures to cope with this problem a fundamental question, here stated in its baldest form, had to be answered concerning whether the offenders were naughty, that is bad but morally responsible, or mentally ill in some way, that is to be treated medically rather than by family or school. It was because both answers seemed right for different young persons that both responses had to be given. But to meet the needs of those seen as mentally ill in some way there was a great expansion and differentiation amongst 'the helping professions' (Halmos, 1970), some of whom were appointed to special positions attached to schools (Musgrave, 1975). In addition, there was a beginning to the demand that moral education should become a school subject (May, 1968, p. 351). Both these responses, at least in theory, could allow the further development of the already mentioned tendency for the family to decline in importance in relation to the school.

Another contemporary social tendency is also relevant at this point. There has been an apparent decline in the interest in and allegiance to formal religion, particularly to Christian churches, in Britain during this century. Increasingly the churches have found it difficult, if not impossible, to give any meaning to the secular life of the times. One side effect of this development, important for this analysis, has been that because religion has had less salience for most people the organized groups who represented it during the discussions leading up to the 1944 Education Act were able to gain a stronger statutory position for religious education in the schools than had been the case under either the 1870 or 1902 Acts (Cannon, 1964). This is an important point in the context and will be taken up in the next chapter when recent developments in religious education are discussed.

In sum, during the years since 1900 changes had taken place in the social structure that fundamentally strengthened the possibility that an alternative morality or, indeed, alternative moralities might develop in Britain. The men of the upper middle class were in power at the turn of the century and their morality was then basically unchallenged so that it was the imposed unitary code of respectability taught, albeit in various versions, in the vast majority of public and state schools. By the thirties their power was not so absolute and after 1945 a government was returned that was at least formally opposed to many of the qualities associated with the old morality. Several other economic and social tendencies were at work to support this change in the social structure. In the context of morality the result was that there was no longer an automatic agreement at the commonsense level on secondary virtues and that from time to time agreement even upon the primary virtues was, perhaps, in some doubt. But British society was by 1950 a basically liberal society. There was a feeling that people should be free to choose for themselves within a broad range of behaviour how they should act. Few tests of belief or of morality were demanded of citizens. It was in this historical setting that in the 1950s a number of influential thinkers began to reconsider the whole area of morality. The result was that around 1960 the phrase, 'the new morality' became common.

The new morality

Individualism

Ralph Turner (1976) has recently pointed out what he sees as a major change in the way in which self-identity is related to society. In early modern times the sense of self seemed to emerge in its strongest form when articulated with social institutions. More recently self-discovery has begun to be discussed in the language of impulse expression. The change has fundamental implications for British education, since the code of morality of the public schools is firmly rooted in the former mode of self-discovery. Those who keep a stiff upper lip do not give way to impulse and are loyal to the institutions they have learnt to serve.

Turner's analysis provides one more way into the concept of a plurality of moral codes which has already been introduced. There are certain aspects of Christianity that can be interpreted in such a way that they match this spirit of plurality. Thus, the commandment, so central to the practical morality of many Christians, 'love your neighbour', can justify behaviour (e.g. pacifism) unsupported by the majority. Furthermore, Protestants have always claimed to support a morality of intention rather than of prescription. Therefore, the way seems open for many to choose for themselves how they will behave towards those whom they claim to love. The concept of self-determination did not seem a very realistic viewpoint to many voters in the mid-nineteenth century when the ballot was still open, or to a member of the working class in the interwar years when jobs were scarce and the power of his representatives at the wage-bargaining table or in parliament was weak. But in the era associated with Harold Macmillan's famous remark, 'We've never had it so good', the belief that one might make real decisions for oneself seemed more credible.

Three widely acclaimed publications, two religious and one secular, covered various aspects of these difficult issues in an influential way in the years soon after 1960. Professor Carstairs gave the BBC's Reith Lectures in 1962 and a published version of them, *This Island Now*, came out in 1963. His analysis was anthropological, and therefore culturally relativistic, but also psychoanalytic, and hence to some extent critical of the reality of free-will. More than anything he wanted to point out that in a society where most people lack religious conviction 'there persists a left-over jumble of ethical precepts, now bereft of their significance' (p. 83). In 1963 the Society of Friends (Quakers) published a pamphlet, *A Quaker View of Sex*, which considered several problems in a very liberal Christian way. The characteristics of this position can best be seen by considering the third of these important works, the then Bishop of Woolwich, John Robinson's book, *Honest to God* (1963), still to this day influential and controversial in both theological and lay circles.

Chapter 6 of *Honest to God* is entitled, 'The New Morality'. This phrase apparently was coined by the Supreme Sacred Congregation of the Holy Office in Rome during 1956 and its tendencies were condemned by that body. Robinson owed much in his consideration of the new morality to the writings of an American theologian, Joseph Fletcher, and summarized his own central position as a support for 'a radical "ethic of the situation" ' (pp. 116–18). His book was seen as extremely relativistic and, despite his disclaimers, as opening the way to possible moral license. As a result he was asked to speak widely and in one series of lectures, given in Liverpool Cathedral late in 1963, expounded his position on contemporary Christian morality very clearly. He was making 'certainly no invitation to license but a plea for the most searching demands of pure personal relationship as the basis of *all* moral judgments' (1964, p. 8). There were 'three polarities in Christian ethics ... fixity and freedom, ... law and love ... authority and experience' (p. 11). He advocated an inductive morality, based on experience to date and on experience in a given situation; this apparently scientific and empirical position appealed to many as in tune with a so-called scientific age. But 'the one thing that finally counts is treating persons as persons with unconditional seriousness' (pp. 36–7). The centrality of inter-personal experience, reported in the last chapter as the central part of the contemporary teenage view of morality, is seen by Robinson as the key to progressive Christianity.

Certainly, this moral stance was a long way from that reported by Durkheim in his lectures to intending school teachers at the turn of the century: 'While all opinions relating to the material world ... are today entitled to free discussion, people do not admit that moral beliefs should be as freely subjected to criti-cisms' (Durkheim, 1961, p. 9).

For Robinson contemporary Christianity was to be discussed and criticized in much the same way as natural science. But the eventual discussion went much farther than many early sup-porters of the new morality might have intended and than many now feel legitimate. Perhaps the extreme position as it relates to education can be seen most easily in *The Little Red School Book*, in which the legitimacy of a morality based upon the authority of adults was challenged on the first page: 'Grown-ups do have a lot of power over you: they are real tigers. But in the long run they can never control you completely: they are paper tigers' (Hansen and Jensen, 1971, p. 9). The individualistic situ-ation ethic, apparently supported by Robinson, was recom-mended in a series of points to 'Remember' which included: 'You are a person in your own right. In the end you're account-able only to yourself. You're as good as anybody else', but which also reminded readers, 'You're not perfect' (p. 74).

A major study of parents of English primary school children car-ried out during the sixties for the Plowden Committee found that

> The great majority of these parents considered that teaching children to behave was a joint responsibility of parents and the schools and did not think that it should be left merely to the teacher. (*Children and their Primary Schools, II*, 1967, p. 135)

A number of comments can be made about this conclusion. Most parents may now see moral education as a joint responsibility, but a century ago it was in the case of many children the sole res-ponsibility of their parents. Furthermore, some parents today, particularly of teenagers, are at a loss to know how to deal with their children and hope that the school will take over the major responsibility.

There is, in addition, considerable evidence to support the view that many parents now see religious education as important in schools not merely to teach belief in any revealed religion, but to impart a basic moral code to their children. Certainly a large study carried out in 1966 by the Schools Council concluded that

> parents very generally considered that the moral training of their children was a very important function of the school ... [Such training was] more widely in demand from parents than youngsters, the differences being particularly great between boys and their parents. (Schools Council, 1968, p. 38)

In the mid-sixties another study found that in the Durham and Newcastle area five out of six parents 'are still in favour of the present legal obligation upon the schools to provide religious education and the support for compulsory daily worship is about as high'. When asked to order suggested reasons as to why children should be taught about Christianity 62·2 per cent ticked 'Christianity is true', but 50·0 per cent also ticked 'It helps people to be good' (May and Johnson, 1967, p. 136). Yet the real problem is that neither teachers nor parents nor, indeed, any of the children's other agents of respectability in the contemporary situation agree what this code of 'goodness' implies. McIntyre has gone further and said:

> The disturbing fact about our society is that we are in just this situation: the effective and honest use of moral predicates does presuppose a shared moral vocabulary in an established moral community, but we do not as a community share such a single moral vocabulary. (1967b, p. 52)

The solution adopted by some educators has been to advocate 'the morality of involvement and discovery (in which) the search itself is the moral education' (Hemming, 1963).

Such a course may leave children in some insecurity as was the girl who wrote 'The Poem of the Confused' quoted on pp. 51–2. They do not know, because no one will tell them, to what standards they should conform. All they know is that they may criticize imposed moral prescriptions. In such a situation of possible moral insecurity adolescents may easily qualify for treatment by counsellors of one type or another since they may have been defined not as naughty, but as mentally ill.

The first administrative measures to implement 'the new philanthropy' were taken at a societal level. For example, in 1907 the School Medical Service was established. Ultimately by around 1950 the structure of the British welfare state had been created. Yet poverty and illness, whether physiological or mental, and particularly the latter, were not eliminated. As a result, and paralleling much that has been said before, there was a switch from analysing problems at the sociological level to thinking at the social-psychological level. An index of this is the extension since the Second World War of the counselling professions; what has been called 'the professionalization of personal helping' (Halmos, 1965, p. 29) took place. These occupational groupings were concerned 'to bring about changes in the body or personality of the client, and, hence, Halmos elsewhere called them 'personal service professions' (1970, p. 22). Two values that were central to their ideology are important here, namely, first, their 'abandonment of judgment and condemnation' of their clients and, second, their 'cultivation of a mutually honest and intimate "I–Thou" relationship between man and man' (p. 19). These values closely parallel the new morality. Furthermore, the belief that the behavioural sciences provided the principal tools for their professional tasks was also growing during this same period.

Halmos has shown how this ideology affected the contemporary view of the teacher's role. There is now a fuller acceptance by teachers of the possibility of unconscious motivation for acts; a less punitive view of sexuality in children; a greater forebearance for aggression against teachers and an attempt to avoid the creation of guilt about such aggression; and a willingness to allow freedom to children to develop to their genetic potential (pp. 101–2). Despite constant complaints, largely true, that few social workers had been trained in the behavioural sciences, more and more teachers were coming into touch during their training with the tradition of progressive education which had grown in the colleges between the wars and which owed much to psychoanalytic modes of thought (Armytage, 1975).

After the war a potentially paradoxical element was built into the developing ideology of the helping professions. A great emphasis came to be put on the place of the family, and especially of the mother, in the upbringing of the child. During the fifties Dr John Bowlby's *Child Care and the Growth of Love* (1951) achieved great influence as a set book in training courses for all the helping professions including teaching. This book was based on work done for the World Health Organization (WHO) on the adverse effects of maternal deprivation upon the mental health of children. It is worth pointing out here that the preamble to the constitution of the WHO contained these words, 'Health is a condition of complete physical, mental and social wellbeing and not just the absence of disease or infirmity.' A very wide remit was claimed and given at the international level to a fundamentally medical body. The British Medical Association (BMA) likewise showed its continuing wide definition of its own role by choosing in 1959–60 as the subject for the year, 'The Adolescent'. The result was a pamphlet, *Medical and Social Aspects of Adolescence* (1961) in which the BMA recommended that it should run courses for parents to help them advise children with more understanding; that family doctors should give more attention to the problems of adolescence; and that the undergraduate training of doctors should prepare them for this role. The paradox was that at the moment when more emphasis was being put upon the family, and particularly the mother, more power was also being claimed by the professionals, the medical men, in saying how parents should enact their role.

There were some reactions, and not just at the lay level, to the swing to medical, more especially psychoanalytic, explanations of what might also be seen as immoral acts. The Chief Medical Officer of the Ministry of Education in his Report for 1954/5 wrote: 'Many maladjusted children are normal children who have just slipped off the rails, and it is, therefore, undesirable to put into their minds or the minds of their parents an idea that they are sick children' (p. 137). There is no sharp cleavage between right and wrong or between sanity and insanity, but now the difficulties in deciding whether a child was a case for doctor or teacher or parent was growing much more complicated because the line between the basic and previously separated categories of morality and sanity were themselves becoming blurred.

Two other series of events around 1960 are symptomatic of this confusion. First, a new tradition of research, based in psychiatry, but to become influential in sociology and social psychology, was born. In 1961 Szasz, an American psychiatrist, wrote his book *The Myth of Mental Illness*. In simple terms his thesis was that mental illness was culture-bound and often those who were sick were so only because they had been labelled as mad. Contemporaneously in London another psychiatrist, R. D. Laing, was developing a radical analysis of the mental illness, schizophrenia. In 1960 he published *The Divided Self*. Laing's argument was that many acts usually seen as insane are in fact quite rational when interpreted 'in the light of the praxis and process of (the) family nexus' (Laing and Esterson, 1964, p. 13). As a result we find the medical men, the acknowledged experts in the field of mental health, arguing amongst themselves and radical members of the profession advocating a more sociological, and less purely physiological, approach to the field.

Meanwhile, the whole field of the British law of lunacy was under consideration. A Royal Commission on the Law relating to Mental Illness and Mental Deficiency was appointed in 1954 and reported in 1957. Legislation based on, but not entirely following the legal definitions of mental illness recommended by the Commission was enacted in 1959. What Dr Summerskill, speaking in the Commons during the debate, called the former 'mediaeval approach to the disturbed mind' (Hansard: vol. 598, col. 727) was replaced; four categories of mental illness were recognized, namely 'mental disorder', 'severe subnormality', 'subnormality' and 'psychopathic disorder'. From 1913 there had been a category of 'moral imbecile'; after 1927 this category was renamed 'moral defective'. However, in the new Mental Health Act (1959) 'promiscuity or other criminal conduct' was explicitly excluded (Sec. 4(1)–(5)). Every attempt was consciously made to equate mental and physical illness in this legislation. Thus, despite Austen Albu's opposition on the grounds that in many cases 'diagnosis is essentially a social judgment' (Hansard: vol. 598, cols. 758–9), lay participation in the procedure for admission to mental hospitals, formerly essential, was now withdrawn in favour of a decision by two experts.

Thus, at the very moment when radical psychiatrists (themselves medically trained) were challenging the right of the doctors to claim expertise in this field – a claim originally successfully made, it will be remembered, only in the 1830's – parliament had legislated in a way that gave medical men absolute legitimacy in the field of mental health. At a time when the new morality had ensured much confusion about morals there was now no doubt who were experts on one side of the murky divide between morality and health.

Chosen, pluralistic moralities: 1960–

No longer was it possible for those in power, whether representing the upper middle and middle classes or the working class, to try to impose one morality on the young through the schools. There could be a plurality of codes available, at least in theory, for the choice of those who were growing up and the task of those responsible for moral education and mental health was to help the young to choose from the available moralities or, perhaps, even to help them to create for themselves a new morality. No longer was it as possible as it had been half a century before for the older generation to impose a code upon the young from a position of authority.

Moral education

There is a tendency to write about the views of adolescents concerning their families as if parents and their children were in constant conflict. However, there is much evidence to show that relationships within the family are more serene than this. Thus, 86 per cent of the children ($N=11,045$) in the British National Child Development Study when asked in 1974 at the age of sixteen to comment on the statement 'I get on well with my mother' replied either 'Very true' or 'true', as did 80 per cent when asked in similar terms about their relationship with their fathers (Fogelman, 1976, p. 36). Yet often because of their parent's partial withdrawal from the position of moral teachers and also because of the increased participation of mothers in the work-force moral education, always on the curricular agenda of British schools, has come to be seen as of major importance. Thus, in 1967 more than 60 per cent of a large national sample of teachers answering a postal questionnaire thought that schools should provide separate periods for moral education (May, 1969, p. 351).

Yet this development occurred at a time when teachers themselves were starting, or wanting, to withdraw from making moral judgments of their pupils. This was probably because an increasing number were trained to hold a professional ideology akin to that of the personal service professions and because, inasmuch as teachers could be seen as members of the intelligentsia, this was a section of society within which the new morality had a wide influence. Furthermore, the growing belief in a child-centred education, often associated with the writings of John Dewey, meant that, especially at the primary level, teachers were sympathetic to the concept of self-development, and this was congruent with the ideal of choosing for oneself. Those who favoured progressive education also usually preferred the use of rewards to punishments as sanctions in school. The decline in physical punishments already reported (Musgrave, 1977a) was probably offset not just by a rise of verbal punishments, but by a switch to rewards. There seemed in addition to be a greater tolerance of minor misdemeanours. The iron hand was no longer used to treat rebels.

Although the moral curriculum of British schools had been characterized by an attempt to impose a unitary code of secondary virtues the versions transmitted in the past have been shown to differ by the type of school concerned. There was a hierarchy of versions that matched the hierarchy of schools. In the public schools a morality of authority and service was taught, in the grammar schools of work and self-help and in the old elementary schools of submission and duty. The establishment of a unitary state system at secondary as well as at primary level was one of the aims embodied in the replacement of a tripartite secondary system by the comprehensive school. This might have led to the transmission of a unitary code of morality. However, diversity between schools has been replaced by a diversity available for choice within one type of secondary school. Perhaps the situation is more complicated in that a diversity based on one set of secondary virtues has not merely given way to a diversity of codes, but possibly even to the questioning of primary virtues, particularly by older pupils.

This diversity in itself might not be socially disadvantageous, but it seems that because there is not yet an agreed grammar of moral discourse upon which to build discussion in moral education pupils may, in extreme cases, be left with doubts about how to think about moral questions. The evidence from a group in their mid-teens which was reported in the last chapter does not give a picture of such insecurity, but it does show a group who were consciously growing into a period of uncertainty. In such circumstances, although some doubts and some insecurity within the bounds of what is socially defined as 'mental health' is inevitable as young persons grow up, one goal of moral education in schools may be seen as the attempt to reduce, not to increase, the difficulties inherent in this process.

Certainly, it is moral, rather than religious, education that increasingly has been seen as the part of the curriculum to which this aim is given. One index of this change is that the journal, formerly called *Religion in Education* changed its name in 1961 to *Learning for Living*. The growth in emphasis on this new subject has led to a demand for experts in it. In an age of specialization a new subject implies a new type of teacher trained to teach it. In addition, there is an implied need for specific curricular materials and, therefore, for experts in curricular development in this field. The Schools Council has financed two projects, the first (McPhail, 1972) for the secondary level and the second, not yet completed, for the junior school. Interestingly McPhail himself was trained as a social psychologist and when in the next chapter we come to examine the nature of contemporary curricula in moral education the influence of the social sciences will be very apparent.

Mental health

As a result of the growing importance of the concept of mental health that was noted above the number of those employed in the personal service professions has greatly increased. Between the 1901 and 1951 Censuses there was a decrease of 54 per cent in the number of people to each medical or paramedical professional (Halmos, 1965, p. 33). The tendency for the mental health of children to be placed more and more in the hands of medical men or of professionals who use medical frameworks of thinking has also continued since the 1960s. Two changes made during the reorganization of the Health Service following upon the National Health Service Reorganization Act of 1973 support this view. The first concerns the School Health Service; from 1974 this service ceased to be the administrative responsibility of the Ministry of Education and was included in the National Health Service, thus coming directly under the control of the Department of Health and Social Security. In 1974 a circular (HRC 27) on Health Education was published by this latter department. This visualized the establishment of Health Education Services in each Health Area under the control of an Area Health Education Officer, a specialist on the staff of the Area Medical Officer whose prime aim would be 'to enable, through educational means, individuals to maintain or, if necessary, improve their health to the maximum possible' (Kay, 1975, p. 99).

It is of significance that Kay sees this service developing along the lines laid down by the WHO Expert Committee on Health Education which reported in 1954. In its report (Wall, 1955) this committee provided a fine example of the application of 'the faith of the counsellors' to education. A healthy response is defined in terms of 'whether it in general brings the child into an acceptable and satisfying relationship with his environment' (p. 25). The nature of this view can be seen more exactly in a further quotation from the same report:

> The process of education is the means by which society specifies acceptable outlets for (the) innate needs and capacities of the individual ar d at the same time ensures that they will enrich his personal life as well as serve his society. (p. 25)

Bantock has traced two other sources of influence upon the development of the concept of mental health as it relates to the school. Starting in the late-fifties a series of conferences was run at Keele University on the implications of theories of personality development for the training of teachers and social workers. Also, in 1959 Professor Ben Morris strongly supported the view that too much emphasis was being put on intelligence in teacher training and in schools; 'mental health (was) largely a matter of the emotions' (Bantock, 1967, pp. 23–30). There were, then, strong forces at work upon teachers and others in the helping professions to bring them to see mental health in terms that related human needs, emotional as well as intellectual, seen in psychological terms, to the demands of a particular society through the adjustment of an individual to his environment.

Increasingly those in the schools were in a position of conflict. They were seen as responsible for and trained for defining success amongst their pupils on academic and moral criteria. However, in the latter case the strict methods of the early part of the century were now unpopular and were being replaced by the softer strategies of control associated with the counselling ideology. The hope was that after receiving counselling 'the client will continue the dialogue, in his solitariness, with an internalized image of the partner-counsellor' (Halmos, 1965, p. 152). The Freudian influence here is clear. The Super-Ego was to be developed to monitor the innate aggression and sexual impulses of the Id in order to support the conscious Ego. Such ideas had become influential amongst progressive educationalists, but the paradox is that, although there is scope here for close control and a new form of the iron hand, relying on a complex psychology rather than on open force, the ideology of tolerance amongst counsellors recognized the mechanism, but tried to leave the actual direction of the decision to be made to the client or pupil concerned. As Bantock (1967, pp. 44–64) has pointed out, the movement towards progressive education also owed much to the Enlightenment's support for rationality as a means of eliminating evil. The

Freudians, however, in supporting the view that the Super-Ego was an unconscious process, were taking a step back from the use of reason.

Once again we can see that there is a dilemma implicit in the view held by many doctors, teachers and counsellors concerning what mental health is. An approach to wrongdoing and to anti-social behaviour that sees the individual as a responsible, creative, rational being will, at least initially, support a form of moral education that teaches children how to decide for themselves about their standards of behaviour and their actions towards others. However, an approach in terms of mental health, perceived according to the medical, or perhaps more accurately, the psychiatric model, will, at least as a starting point, define the deviant as a patient or a client who is sick.

Conclusion

From the account given in this chapter there appears to have been a move from a situation where both the state-provided and the public schools, especially those for boys, were involved in an attempt to teach a consensual, deferential morality. Somewhat different versions of the moral code of the upper middle class were taught in a hierarchy of school types that matched the levels of the social classes at the time. Criticism of this code did, however, develop. Initially it was not radical in any sense, but when the economic and political structures of the country changed there was the possibility of a total change in the code of morality that was basic to the moral curriculum of British schools. The basis of morality in Christianity has also become less widely accepted, but no real replacement for one code, rooted in a revealed religion, has yet been suggested, nor indeed is advocated, despite, or perhaps because of, the attempts by various denominations to come to grips with a 'new morality'.

Moral education has gained a place as a school subject and experts in this new specialism can now be found. What is of importance is to try to discover who are the agents of respectability for the codes of morality that now exist and may be transmitted in the schools through this subject or through any other part of the curriculum. It may be that different dimensions of behaviour are sanctioned by different agents of respectability. Certainly medical men have played a changing role in this respect. Initially they had their effect through their control over matters relating to physiological medicine whereas more recently mental health has become the main field for their influence in the moral context. Parents have begun to hand moral power to teachers, though the data reported in the last chapter make clear that teenagers now do not themsleves see teachers as important figures for moral advice.

During a period when codes of morality are of uncertain nature, agents of respectability also seem difficult to locate. This development has occurred at a time when some experts have recommended self-discovery and responsible choice as the ways to morality, whilst others have emphasized the need for security, particularly in the family, during a child's upbringing. But such moral security, we have seen in the last chapter, probably cannot often survive adolescence. Authority in moral matters is today often unacceptable and much criticized. Yet it may well be that moral codes, as Durkheim indicated, depend upon an element of authority. It is to this type of issue that we must turn in the final chapter. First of all, however, the intention is to consider in more detail how the developments outlined in this chapter have affected both the teaching of the various relevant school subjects and also some of the facets of school organization that can be directly associated with the moral curriculum.

5

The changing elements of the moral curriculum

> The easy and ever-repeated reading of that sacred classic of the whole world, the Bible, for instance, will make any capable person not only 'wise unto salvation' ... but also lettered, cultivated, refined beyond 'the guess of folly'.
>
> (S. Brown, *Itinerating Libraries and their Founder*, 1856, p. 15)

Those in schools may plan to pass on the moral curriculum solely through the formal teaching of academic subjects, but since the organization of any school is easily open to structuring with some conscious aim in view many attempts to inculcate moral lessons are made by organizing schools in some special way (Sugarman, 1968). Therefore, before examining the ways in which the relevant school subjects have developed since the turn of the century we shall rather briefly consider some aspects of school organization.

School organization and the moral curriculum

During the early twenties, and even into the thirties *The Loom of Youth* was still thought of as an attack on the public schools, but its account of the organizational methods of teaching the moral code of the upper middle class remained a reasonably accurate one. Chapel, games and the corps were all compulsory; the perfect system and fagging were supposed to inculcate a spirit of service, obedience and responsibility. These schools were not co-educational, but in those for girls the pupils learned a code somewhat the same as that taught in the boys' schools.

Today the public schools still have immense power and are in great demand from their traditional clientele or from those who aspire to the status of the upper middle class for their children. But although the elements of the old organization are still there the emphasis is now rather different. Prize days remain. Prefects are sometimes elected rather than appointed by the head. There is often a choice between the games to be played, not all of which will be team games. Chapel may be compulsory solely for younger pupils or compulsory only on certain occasions, whilst for the older pupils the option of not attending may be genuinely open. There is still a school corps, but there may also be the chance to choose to take part in a programme of social service instead. Co-education has become not common, but at least is found occasionally amongst these schools. The older forms of fagging have disappeared, and prefects tend to be seen less as learning to exercise power, but rather as taking a social responsibility for younger pupils (Hansen, 1974). In brief, the organization for teaching the moral code has a somewhat similar structure to what it had fifty years ago, but new, though similar elements, have been added to meet the recent emphasis upon choice, the wider tolerance of differences and the greater importance of the individual in relation to any social claims on him.

Clearly the room for change in the state-provided schools, particularly from the position exemplified by the older elementary schools, was great. When teachers had classes of fifty and the Elementary Code was still an instrument of close curricular control situations such as that in a London school during the early-1900s, here described in retrospect by a very sensitive writer, cannot have been uncommon:

In front of his desk, as a kind of altar, stood a long chest, open during school hours to reveal a set of canes of varying thickness and colour from light switches to heavy cudgels; some straw blond, others dour as mahogany as though impregnated with congealed blood. Lying on the array of canes was the

Punishment Book, the register of shame. (R. Church, *Over the Bridge*, 1955, p. 134)

The analysis of these 'registers of shame' already cited (Musgrave, 1977a) indicates, it will be remembered, that girls as well as boys and infants as well as older children were given corporal punishment for a wide range of offences in addition to those concerned with the academic curriculum, that is for classroom misbehaviour or bad work. Lack of punctuality, particularly in rural schools, was a common offence (7·3 per cent of offences during 1900–39); bad manners or bad language, including irreverence – and not only in church schools – was not uncommon (3·3 per cent); uncleanliness, including 'going unwashed', 'dirty hands', or 'dirty boots' were not infrequent causes of corporal punishment, though far less so after the First World War (1·8 per cent). Disobedience and insubordination outside the classroom were much more common reasons (12·2 per cent) and lack of consideration for others or their property was the main moral offence punished (15·8 per cent); in addition, a small number of pupils were punished for lying or cheating (2·5 per cent). Here we can clearly see the negative sanctions involved in trying to teach a morality of deference, 'good habits' of work and obedience. About positive sanctions or rewards we can only surmise that praise and the encouraging look were sometimes used.

In 1948–9 a large representative sample (N = 724) of teachers in England and Wales responded to a questionnaire concerning their attitudes towards and their practices regarding punishment and rewards. 89·2 per cent agreed that corporal punishment should be retained in schools as a last resort and 77·8 per cent were strongly in favour of corporal punishment used with discretion; men and older teachers were more in favour than women and younger teachers (Highfield and Pinsent, 1954, pp. 279–91). In another part of this same study the majority of teachers were found to define 'misdemeanours as acts contrary to school regulations'; this was less so amongst women teachers, whether in primary or secondary schools, who saw misdemeanours 'as acts indicative of low standards of conduct, and of disordered personality which needed psychological investigation and treatment rather than summary punishment' (p. 253). This evidence seems to show the lingering strength of the harsh code of the early years of the century, but also to indicate both the early influence of the mental health movement and the growth of a belief associated with the progressive movement that rewards were in general more efficacious than punishments in teaching the moral curriculum, however necessary the latter form of sanction might be on occasion.

Very recently evidence has become available about the practices of primary schools. By the 1970s there were few teachers in these schools who had not been trained since the influence of progressive methods had become more powerful in English primary education. In his study of primary schools (N=37) in north-west England Bennett has reported that 'discipline does not appear to be a problem at the primary level' (1976, p. 44). Less than one in ten of teachers (N=468) claimed to have many pupils who created disciplinary problems and over 95 per cent found that verbal reproof was normally sufficient punishment to cope with a difficulty. However, over half these teachers did admit to smacking children occasionally despite the fact that this was frowned upon at the official level.

Smaller classes, more apt methods and materials have made primary schools more interesting places for children so that their attention wanders less. But though the range of behaviour tolerated may be wider and deference is probably no longer so central to the moral code now taught in these schools many of the same old lessons may well be inculcated more efficiently by the new methods. A lack of consideration for others, dishonesty and insubordination may be less often provoked in smaller classes with a kind and tolerant teacher. In addition, the system more frequently practised of rotating positions of responsibility amongst pupils allows all to bear some responsibility and does not merely allow one set of children, often the same ones throughout a school year to gain these important experiences. From the evidence cited in Chapter 3 we may deduce that primary children generally still accept without criticism a moral code taught by their elders. It is at the secondary level that questioning begins.

Initially each part of the tripartite system imitated the code of morals and the methods of teaching it that they inherited from the nineteenth-century boys' public schools. A number of studies of different types of school have documented this. King (1969) has shown how the teachers of a grammar school in south-east England defined the content of the moral code that they wished to pass on to their pupils. Service to others, at the possible expense of monetary reward, and hard work, if necessary involving the deferral of present enjoyment, were important virtues. Unfortunately for the staff this descendant of the middle-class version of the public school code received lukewarm support from the pupils of the school who had a very much more instrumental view of their studies and a tendency to support the immediate gratification of pleasures. Taylor (1963) looked at the way in which secondary modern schools were developing up to 1960 before the growth in numbers of comprehensive schools. He showed how these schools had imitated the grammar, and hence indirectly the public schools, largely in an attempt to raise their status in the eyes of the general public. They had, therefore, adopted such elements of organization as prefects, school uniform and compulsory games that were seen to play a very important part in the moral curriculum.

There have been few studies of the content or organization of the moral curriculum in comprehensive schools. One early work (Miller, 1961) traced the way in which the academic curriculum of the grammar and modern schools was maintained within the one new type of secondary school. From this study which also investigated some of the values held by the pupils in one comprehensive school it was apparent that those values that tend to control behaviour towards others and that are usually associated with the social classes who were in the majority in the organizationally separate grammar and modern schools were represented within the upper and lower stream of the comprehensive school in much the same way that might have been predicted. However, we need to have much firmer evidence before generalizing about the moral curriculum of this type of school.

Comprehensive schools are often so large that there are thought to be enough problem children in them to appoint counsellors to their staffs. Indeed, in Scotland establishments and staff grades have been altered to make this possible. These counsellors sometimes work with pupils who have problems of a personal or academic nature, but moral problems tend to take up much of their time, especially during their regular lessons with 'normal' children. Whilst much benefit may come from this new way of organizing part of the moral curriculum there are disadvantages that are implicit in the presently expected behaviour of teachers and counsellors. Teachers are concerned with achieving academic and moral results in their pupils and when the standards seen as 'right' in their school are not achieved sanctions are applied. Counsellors, however, try to avoid such a judgmental stance. Pupils expect teachers, whether of chemistry or counselling, to behave as teachers. If they find, for example, that the first teacher punishes whilst the second does not, conflict may follow for teachers and pupils alike. It is in part for such reasons, but also to try to improve efficiency in delivering the very varied specialist services now available, that in some local education authorities (LEAs) teams of experts with various skills are attached to groups of schools with the same aim of dealing with problems, often of a moral nature, that teachers see as beyond their pedagogical expertise, but within the competence of persons who have a basically medical outlook (Musgrave, 1975).

The Little Red School Book said that 'policy should be decided democratically' (Hansen and Jensen, 1971, p. 40). Some schools have tried to introduce school councils in order to give their pupils a chance to learn that they have to tolerate the views of others, co-exist with those with whom they differ and to give them experiences of making decisions which are mainly moral in nature. Often such councils have failed in their aims because they have been given no power over decisions that will really alter what happens in schools. More recently Ungoed-Thomas has pointed out that many pupils ought, and in fact do, have the opportunity to learn these moral lessons by participating 'as members of form or tutorial groups, of year or houses, of clubs and societies, of the prefects, or indeed of the whole school' (1972, pp. 1–2).

Here we are reminded that the manner in which a school is organized can have a powerful influence upon the ways in which teachers and pupils treat each other. The moral curriculum must aim to influence social behaviour now and in the future. Hence, the style of interpersonal relationships in any school becomes one crucial factor that can be varied. The style of teaching can be important. Traditional teachers rarely claim to impart moral lessons through their style, but when they do they would probably claim that the lessons would in general relate to authority and deference. Many progressive teachers do make the claim that their style releases their pupils from such lessons; for example, those who support 'open' classrooms sometimes claim, what observation seems to confirm, that the hostility that can be generated in the direct confrontation of a traditional classroom is dissipated in the open classroom where easier relationships are possible between teacher and pupils, and between pupils and pupils so that learning to live with one's own and the older generation can be more easily achieved. Even in traditionally run schools some attempts have been made to produce a similar result by organizing school trips or camps, usually – and this is an important index of the way the matter has been viewed – held in school holidays and away from the school itself. In addition, easy mixing between pupils has always been encouraged in British schools through various forms of extracurricular activity, including participation in clubs and societies.

Since Baden-Powell, himself newly returned from the Boer War, introduced scouting in the first decade of this century, a period seminal for many parts of the moral curriculum, the existence of a Scout or Guide troop in a school has been seen as essentially an agent of moral education. Personal responsibility, honesty, determination, sexual purity and religious belief, Christian originally, but eventually of any faith, are encouraged by a system based on ritual pressures, a graduated progression matching the socially defined stages of growth in boys and girls, a highly regarded uniform, outdoor living and a stress on self-discipline. The aims implicit in the Scout law and promises, or their equivalents for Guides, have not changed though the means of teaching them have altered somewhat to meet social pressures (Orr, 1963).

The school corps which was almost a *sine qua non* of the public school, but which was also found in many grammar schools, has very similar aims to the Scouts but provides a military and more authoritarian setting. In addition, in most British secondary schools there are many clubs or societies and activities such as school plays or excursions, whose existence is justified in terms which are often moral in nature. Thus, in the thirties the Chief Medical Officer of the Board of Education saw Red Cross Links, of which in 1935 there were 350 in England and Wales, many associated with schools, as important because they 'encouraged the habits of healthy living', helped 'the sick and suffering' and formed 'a chain of service linking the youth of all lands' (*Report*, 1935, p. 63).

Since 1950 the growth in the emphasis on the individual, on voluntariness and on choice has led to a wider range of opportunities for such activities, but one development in itself indicates most of these changes, namely the growth of the Duke of Edinburgh's Award Scheme. This began in 1956, initially for boys, but in 1958 was extended to girls, and in many cases local arrangements for administering the Award were based on schools. The Award is granted at three levels, but the basic conditions for award are similar for both sexes at each level and are dependent upon passing certain reasonable standards of physical fitness including participation in an outdoor expedition, demonstrating over time competence in interests or pursuits of one's own choice, and, finally, undertaking a period of service to others (Carpenter, 1966). Within this broad framework there is the possibility to show individuality; in addition, persistence, endurance, adventurousness, consideration to others and competence to help others are all moral qualities that the scheme aims to encourage. This code could almost function as a secular and individual contemporary version of the old public school ethic rooted as it is in leisure activities rather than in work.

School subjects and the moral curriculum

Religious education
Religious education was not required by law in schools in England and Wales by the Education Act of 1870 and 1902. The general assumption was that it would be given, and where it was the law ensured that the content would be Christian, but non-denominational. Most LEAs did lay down a very brief syllabus. By the 1920s, as the temperature of religious debate dropped, more detailed agreement between denominations about what should be taught became possible. In 1924 *The Cambridgeshire Syllabus of Religious Teaching for Schools* was published and seemed to start a national movement towards such arrangements. By 1934, 224 out of 316 LEAs had adopted such syllabuses of which 40 were in circulation. Eighty-seven LEAs had, however, adopted *The Cambridgeshire Syllabus* (Hull, 1975, pp. 98–9).

The Cambridgeshire Syllabus was seen as an enlightened exemplar of religious education and its influence continued after the 1944 Education Act which enacted that 'The school day in every county school ... shall begin with collective worship on the part of all pupils ... (and that) religious instruction shall be given in every county school' (Sec. 25). In addition, a procedure was laid down in Schedule V of the Act whereby LEAs should convene a conference of representatives of religious interests that would prepare or adopt an agreed syllabus. The early versions of the influential *Cambridgeshire Syllabus* were basically syllabuses of religious instruction, not of moral education. It was clear, however, that there were moral implications in such passages as, 'Duty to God and man, that is religion. To know God is eternal life, that is theology ...' (1929, p. 2). The 1939 revision, though still largely a detailed syllabus, did allow more freedom to teachers, particularly concerning how they ran school assembly. Furthermore, in one passage the moral lessons of school organization were emphasized, 'The whole ordering of the school can and should contribute to religious instruction in the wider sense' (1939, p. 9). There was also the realization that moral habits were influenced by the environment especially of the nursery school (p. 17); amongst older children 'questioning of conduct and problems about God' were seen as 'natural' (p. 51). By 1949 the emphasis on the quality of interpersonal relationship to be found in the 1939 edition was more pronounced (1949, p. 19).

In Scotland the teaching of religious instruction had, perhaps because of the predominance of Presbyterianism, been less problematic. The separate Education Acts for Scotland were based on the continuance of 'use and wont', though in 1918 a joint committee of the teachers' organization and the main Protestant churches was established to develop syllabuses (*Moral and Religious Education*, 1972, pp. 128–9). However, by the 1970s only 23 per cent of schools claimed to be following syllabuses prescribed by this joint committee or by their LEA; and no Scottish LEA made any recommendations on moral education (p. 13). Though not perhaps as strongly as in England and Wales the situation in the 1950s was characterized by a move towards establishing mechanisms for agreed syllabuses which, though the *moral* implications of revealed religion were recognized, basically contained details of the content and methods to be used in *religious* instruction.

In 1966 the West Riding LEA issued *Suggestions for Religious Education* which allowed much freedom of material and method to teachers, but in 1968 the Inner London Education Authority went further, clearly indicating the new emphasis by the title of their syllabus, *Learning for Life*; the focus was on moral, rather than religious education. Developments in two other LEAs show very clearly how far the concept of an agreed syllabus has now been pushed. In Bath in 1969 the existing syllabus was withdrawn; no new syllabus was drawn up, but teachers were left to devise their own. However, a loose-leaf handbook was issued; this was to contain an introductory statement together with conference and working papers as they were published by the LEA. Clearly there is now in this city an agreed situation where no syllabus exists and in which material relating to religious instruction does not go through the Education Committee. In addition, the humanists were consulted, though, as Bath has no large community of migrants, it was not seen as necessary to consult their representatives. During 1970 in Birmingham, a city with a large migrant community, a conference was convened which included Christians, Jews, Sikhs, Hindus and Mohammedans. A brief syllabus and detailed optional courses were prepared. The plan was that one religion, chosen from a number, should be studied in depth; in addition two non-religious 'stances', Humanism and Communism, were to be covered in less detail. It was on this last point that this syllabus of *religious* education foundered, since the Conservatives on the council objected to the inclusion of Communism. The issue was referred to the legal authorities and eventually to the Minister, who ruled that the syllabus did not meet the requirements of the 1944 Act. But obviously religious education is now coming to cover a much wider area including both non-Christian faiths and ethical systems without any basis in revelation. Furthermore, the teacher himself may no longer believe in what he is teaching (Hull, 1975).

All these syllabuses rest on an assumption, which may be stated in Sadler's words, written in 1908, namely 'the power of the religious lessons to inspire a high moral ideal and to touch the springs of conduct' (1908, p. xlvii). The relevant research does not support such a position. Thus, experimental measures of resistance to temptation do not show that membership of religious organizations supports such resistance (Wright, 1971, p. 62). Furthermore, though high and current commitment to a religious group may 'reduce the incidence of serious antisocial acts' it has 'no influence over the occurrence of milder delinquencies' (p. 70). Yet, we have already noted McPhail's (1972) evidence that his programme of moral education appeared to influence the behaviour of some adolescents. There seems room for thought concerning which material and methods do have the effect at which schools are aiming in this field.

What is clear is that the mechanism whereby syllabuses in religious education are agreed can now rightly be described as 'an institutionalization of confusion' (McIntyre, 1967b, p. 36). The teaching of religion cannot be cut off from other teaching or from life in general as it was to a great extent under the 1944 Act. Valiant attempts to break out of the present situation, essential in view of the social influences now at work on the schools, are probably in conflict with the law, though the discussions follow-

98

ing from this dilemma may help to clarify the real issues, legal and educational, and also begin to establish an agreed vocabulary which will enable a move towards some rational solution.

Physical education

In 1895 physical education (PE) became a subject eligible for grant for schools on the Elementary Code. The attitudes displayed by the Education Department at the time indicated that in their eyes the main aim of teaching PE was to improve discipline and in practice the subject often assumed the form of drill. In 1900 the new Board of Education allowed organized games as a suitable alternative to drill or physical exercises. However, the lack of suitable playing fields or even of an adequate playground, especially in urban areas, was a major constraint upon the rapid development of games, and even of PE, in the elementary schools. This position may be compared with that in public schools where organized games, played on well-equipped grounds, were a central part of the curriculum, but PE far less common. The revelations of the poor physique of many who tried to enlist during the Boer War led to a reconsideration of the place of PE in the elementary schools. In 1902 the War Office, for a brief period, took the responsibility for preparing a syllabus in PE, but Morant's reorganization inspired a more liberal approach in *The Handbook* of 1905; organized games were encouraged on similar grounds to those that were used to justify them in the public schools. In 1909 a new syllabus was issued, 10,000 copies of which were sold in a year. In it much lip service was given to educational ideas, but the 'real drive was towards therapeutic exercises' (McIntosh, 1968, p. 159).

At the start of the First World War once again there was a cry for military drill in schools, which the Medical Branch of the Board, then in charge of PE, fought off with the words:

> The principal needs for children of this age are the inculcation of habits of discipline and obedience on the one hand, and the promotion of all round physical development on the other. [The official syllabus] provides all that is necessary or desirable. (Board of Education Report, 1913–14: 64)

Such a position, strongly held by George Newman whose long reign as the Chief Medical Officer of the Board lasted from 1907 until 1936, was the main influence on PE until the years immediately following 1945. The unchanging nature of Newman's view is made very obvious in these words from one of his later annual reports:

> It is an inspiring sight, and one which augurs well for the future of the English people, to see the children of the ordinary elementary school, small or large, urban or rural, lined up in the playground practising the art of maintaining their bodies and minds in disciplined vigour. (*Report of Chief Medical Officer*, 1930, p. 69)

In its discussion of physical training (PT) *The Handbook* of 1946 named amongst 'the desirable qualities in the future citizen self control, self respect, courage, decision, good temper,' all of which could be learnt through organized PT and games (p. 163).

After the late forties, however, a changed spirit was to be discerned. In 1952 the Ministry issued a new syllabus *Moving and Growing* in which the influence of Laban's ideas on movement and dance could be clearly seen. In the primary age range boys and girls could do PE together now; the concept of 'training' gave way to that of 'development' and this might differ in rate and scope in each individual. (McIntosh, 1968, p. 262). This emphasis on individual activity was also strong at the secondary level where team games began to be replaced by individual sports so that there was a blurring of the distinction between education and recreation. Furthermore, the whole competitive atmosphere associated with 'the school team winning' had so far changed that the Chief Medical Officer of the Ministry, who was since 1945 no longer in charge of PE, could write in the late fifties:

> It is easier for [children] to be adventurous ... in an atmosphere in which there is as little measuring up as possible, which is not too much conditioned by rewards, and where the honour of the group is not always at stake. (*Report of Chief Medical Officer*, 1958–9, pp. 119–20)

There had been a movement in accordance with changing ideological positions outside education from drill to therapy and then to an emphasis on self-discovery and an awareness of the developing body. Blind obedience had given way to the opportunity, at least on occasion, to show initiative. Character training through competitive team games had in part been replaced by the opportunity to develop oneself as an individual. The effect of these changes on the public schools is somewhat doubtful. Public schools for girls had never been so extreme in the pursuit of athleticism as boys' schools, but the latter had moved away from an almost total emphasis on compulsory team games towards a greater use of PE and individual sports. Yet in these schools the competitive element was still strong and the term 'movement' was rarely heard (McIntosh, 1968, pp. 283–4).

Health education

Around 1900 a subject called hygiene was taught in some schools although unpopular amongst teachers as it was 'confused with fads, statistics, and home nursing' (Sadler, 1908, p. 260). The opportunity presented by the reorganization that followed the establishment of the School Medical Service in 1907 was grasped by Newman for an attempt to improve the quality and to extend the influence of what was taught in the schools under this heading. New syllabuses were published. The first was on hygiene in 1907 and this was extended in 1909 by the addition of a *Syllabus on Temperance*; the aims of both can be judged from the declared aim of the latter, namely 'to supply ... plain reasons for the good habits' to be developed in home and school. In addition, a circular was issued in 1910 on the Teaching of Infant Care to Girls. In his *Report for 1911* Newman commented that

> the schools ... afford the best practical means of training the working class mother to take care of her child. Stress should be laid on the need ... to train the child at an early age in good habits of the mind and body. (pp. 233–4)

The 'good habits' were listed in more detail in the Circular and included neatness, cleanliness, table manners and thrift (Musgrave, 1977c).

The Medical Branch of the Board saw its remit and its competence as wide:

> For our business is not only to instruct the child or the adolescent and provide him with information on Hygiene, a body of knowledge, but to teach him actually *how to live*, at the top of his capacity, avoiding the evil and choosing the good. (*Report of Chief Medical Officer*, 1919, p. 171; italics in original)

The branch also realized that conditions varied from school to school. In a paper concerning the teaching of mothercraft to girls

101

the importance of local conditions was emphasized in these words, 'It would be unnecessary, for example, in a well-to-do neighbourhood to suggest the possible transformation of banana boxes into cradles ...' (Musgrave, 1977c).

What effects did Newman's morally laden syllabuses have? In 1907 an HMI had reported 'Elaborate lessons are given in cleanliness in schools where no paper is supplied or used in the closets.' In 1930 Newman reported that in about a third of boys' senior elementary schools there was no systematic instruction in hygiene (*Report*, 1930, pp. 47–9) and in 1936 'in one school of 350 children, although they had seven copies of *The Handbook*, they had only one towel' (*Report*, 1936, p. 82). Why were the results so meagre? Newman thought that this was due to the fact that health education was not really part of the British curricular tradition and so was not regarded as important; furthermore, it was not easily examinable; but, crucially, it touched directly on the home, often in a way that could be seen as critical of what parents did (*Report*, 1929, pp. 50–1). As a result of the obvious lack of success of the syllabuses to date Newman initiated during his last years in office a reconsideration of the relevant courses in schools and, in an attempt to improve the teaching of the subject, in teachers' colleges. *The Handbook of Suggestions*, issued in 1933, contained a chapter on 'Health Education' which included three sections: health and the individual, health and the school, health and the community. The first section incorporated much of the material from the former pamphlets *The Hygiene of Food and Drink*, which was a direct descendant of the old syllabus on 'Temperance', and *The Teaching of Infant Care and Management*. This *Handbook* was reissued in 1945 and the phrase, 'the importance of forming healthy habits' (p. 161) was still there.

However, in 1956 the Ministry produced a separate pamphlet on *Health Education*. In this there was a wider coverage despite the retention of the three sections of the 1933 Handbook. The front of this pamphlet carried a picture of a sculpture by Henry Moore, 'The Family', presumably intended to symbolize a major new direction in the teaching of the subject. The contents were perhaps more resonant of Spock than of Freud, but the account of normal development, the emphasis on early childhood and on interpersonal relationships especially, but not only, within the family do offset the expected material based on biology. The advice offered to teachers about sex education does owe much more to the biological sciences than to any theories of a psychological nature despite the fact that 'a brief review of at least some aspects of mental health' was also seen as 'essential' (p. 156). This pamphlet was revised and reissued in 1968, though in a form little changed from the earlier edition.

A number of textbooks for teachers were also published during this period. Bibby (1951) included two pages (pp. 43–5) on mental health as such and in the appendices where curricula were considered in detail there were some references to the moral qualities which a school might aim to teach (pp. 125–31). The remaining material was largely biological in nature. There was a somewhat similar emphasis certainly in the first edition (1962) of the perhaps more influential book by Pirie and Dalzell-Ward, *A Textbook of Mental Health*. There was a brief chapter on 'Mental Health' of four pages and a rather longer account of education for family life which ran to fourteen pages. The second edition (1975) did, however, show a changed emphasis since it contained chapters on 'Mental Health' (nine pages), on 'Preparation for marriage and family life' (ten pages), 'Parentcraft' (ten pages) and on 'Matters of public concern' (thirty-seven pages), including birth-control, smoking, alcohol and sexually transmitted diseases; in other words, almost one fifth of the book was given to the social side of the subject.

There is little evidence to show what is actually being taught in schools, or what children learn from this subject. One recent study was based on retrospective reports by college students in their first year concerning what they were taught in their secondary schools. Because of the nature of this sample it was, perforce, unrepresentative, being drawn mainly from grammar schools. The conclusion, however, does reinforce the impression given by studying syllabuses and textbooks: '... the anatomical content of health education was shown to be considerable, whereas the social/moral side failed to command an equivalent emphasis' (Morant, 1971, p. 57). The survey also indicated that the latter type of topic was dealt with too late to influence many pupils. In addition, many of the traditional school subjects were found to serve as media for teaching Health Education, especially biology, religious instruction and domestic science.

One aspect of the subject, namely sex education, has always been associated with biology and exemplifies in an extreme form one of the difficulties upon which Newman had commented. It is a topic that deeply implicates the family in particular, but more generally the world outside the school. Much contemporary advertising relies upon sexual stimulation and for this reason alone sex education has been seen by many people as increasingly important. Until the Second World War the Board was very reticent about including this topic in the curriculum. In *Suggestions* (1905) the only mention appears under the passage on Elementary Science: 'Human Physiology – a subject unsuitable for detailed treatment in school' (p. 17). Early in 1914 the Board became peripherally involved, up to ministerial level, in the case of a Derbyshire woman teacher who had taught some physiological facts about reproduction to girls aged eleven to thirteen What was very clear in this affair was the strength of parental feeling against such teaching and the wariness which the Board exhibited (Musgrave, 1977c). The 1927 and 1937 *Handbooks* both carried the words, '... anything in the way of ambitious instruction in physiology should be avoided' (pp. 421 and 162). The Chief Medical Officer, however, did plead for discussion of 'the great problem of sex hygiene' in connection with nature study (*Report*, 1919, p. 171).

It was only in 1943 as a result of wartime pressures that the Board, at least in England and Wales, officially pressed for change in this aspect of the curriculum by issuing Pamphlet 119, *Sex Education in Schools and Youth Organizations*. More recently the social problems created by sex and also by smoking and drugs have become so prominent that the Chief Medical Officer has tried to offset the new balance by emphasizing 'that these topics are only part of a health education programme' (*Report*, 1971–2, p. 48). Little is known of the numbers of such courses. But in the early 1970s in Scotland, where for cultural reasons a more restricted coverage may be the case than in England, there was no specific sex education for older pupils in 90 per cent of the primary schools; in secondary schools 48 per cent of girls and 57 per cent of boys did not receive any sex education. A study of what Scottish secondary pupils wanted from health education showed that there was a greater demand for topics 'classified under the broad heading of Sex, Love and Marriage' than for more biological or physiological topics (*Moral and Religious Education*, pp. 15 and 22).

Health education has become a wider subject than hygiene was and it does now give the opportunity, though this seems not widely grasped, for covering the social aspects of health. The problem has become who shall teach it. Shall it be teachers? and if so, of what subject? or parents, doctors or members of the counselling professions? At one level those with a medical training still have much control over content, and this tendency may increase if the plans already mentioned to develop the subject under the aegis of the National Health Service are carried through. The best way to conceptualize what is happening in health education is to see it as a subject still in the process of establishment; its 'paradigm' is still not firm and the interested parties are still struggling for power.

Academic subjects

The more traditional school subjects have often been seen as having an important part to play in the moral curriculum. Biology has been mentioned above in connection with health education. Here we shall examine English and history, and also some of the recent movements to offer integrated versions of such traditional single subjects.

In the late-nineteenth century the teaching of English in the elementary schools was largely a matter of ensuring minimal literacy for those who would leave at twelve years of age. In the public schools work in the Classics was seen to cover many of the literary aims that it was hoped the teaching of English would meet elsewhere. However, as the leaving age was raised and as school classes grew smaller, teachers of English claimed wider aims. Thus, in *The Handbook* of 1937, as reprinted in 1946, the following passage, deeply moral in its implications, appears:

> Literary education is, after all, a systematic attempt to build up a sense of values, to persuade the mind to accept certain types of experiences which are of cultural and personal significance; it is a method of retraining in activity our tradition and characteristic modes of feeling and thinking that have given our civilization its distinctive flavour and direction, but which are in danger of disappearing under the conditions of modern life. (p. 353)

This type of cultural approach to English can be traced back to the writings of Matthew Arnold – HMI, poet and literary critic. He believed in putting the young in touch with the best of literature, especially poetry, as this would, he felt, form their characters and, thereby, influence their actions. This view was strongly represented in the Newbolt Committee's Report on English of 1921 (Mathieson, 1975). But it was developed and spread most of all through the writings of F. R. Leavis, a Cambridge don and critic, and particularly through the journal *Scrutiny* which Leavis ran from 1933 to 1959 (Musgrave, 1973b).

Leavis was concerned to preserve much in our culture that he felt was being undermined by contemporary political and economic trends. He made central to his educational perspective the dictum that 'To set up as a critic is to set up as a judge of values.' As he said, 'A discipline of the reasons for the choice of words ... can become an introduction to the theory of all choices' (p. 259). Together with David Thompson he produced an extremely influential textbook for schools, *Culture and Environment: The Training of Critical Awareness* (1933), in which there were chapters on, amongst other topics, advertising, mass production, levelling down and 'the organic community'. The intention was to teach children to apply the techniques of literary criticism to their considerations of the environment. They were to discriminate in the environment and in their moral behaviour as they did amongst literary works. The type of course in English embodied in this work has become very common in secondary schools since the war, particularly under such titles, now usually associated with integrated approaches to learning, as 'general' or 'modern subjects'. Leavis himself was, and still is, vitally concerned with the part language plays in passing on 'our spiritual, moral and emotional tradition, which preserves the picked experience of ages regarding the finer issues of life' (p. 259). He advocated the teaching of English literature at tertiary level in a way that involved social, political, economic and intellectual development. English would be a contemporary humanist education that would replace the classics. Indeed, his approach was relevant to the literature of any language so that the moral element would be emphasized in all literary studies, certainly beyond the initial mechanical levels, as had supposedly been the case with the classics, though from the evidence of school stories we know that few pupils passed to the higher levels.

English was seen as a separate school subject in elementary schools earlier than was history. Trethewey (1974) has shown how in the colony of Victoria in the middle of the nineteenth century history texts were merely another type of reading book. However, the heroes depicted or the stories told could be used to point up the moral qualities desired in children. Just as love is the central quality associated with many New Testament stories used today in primary schools, so such culturally important qualities as bravery and patriotism were seen as important in the closing

106

years of the nineteenth century. In its discussion of history *The Handbook of Suggestions* in 1946 carried this passage concerning its moral effect on children:

> ... it is a record writ large of [the] influence [of real men and women] for good or evil ... Without any laboured exhortations [pupils] will feel the splendour of heroism, the worth of unselfishness and loyalty, and the meanness of cruelty and cowardice; and the influence of their lessons in history will be at work long after the information imparted to them has been forgotten. (p. 403)

Since the years before the First World War history has been seen in the words of a report of the London County Council to be 'an indispensable element in the training of a citizen' that would teach 'a sense of duty' to society (Rogers, 1961, pp. 18–19), but, as in Victoria, the moral uses to which history has been put have altered throughout the period as the emphases in the culture concerned have changed. In Victoria citizenship and patriotism had the Imperial flavour which those in power in the Education Department wished to stress until as late as 1939; more recently history has given way in Victorian primary schools to social studies and the textbooks used by the mid-1950s exhibited a more purely Australian character (Trethewey, 1974). In England there seems to have been a shift from emphasizing personal moral qualities early in the century towards, by the 1950s, putting an equal stress on the worth of the heritage and on citizenship, (Rogers, 1961, pp. 154–60). Yet even in this latter period there was still a strong emphasis on personal qualities and on the help that a study of history might give to the making of moral judgments. The balance may well now be tipping once again away from the teaching of social lessons and towards the development of the individual.

Once again this whole curricular programme is based upon the assumption that such teaching does affect moral judgments and actions. We have very little work to tell us how true such an assumption is. One study has shown that both eleven and thirteen year olds at one comprehensive school were able to make moral judgments on historical narratives; the older children were more able to do so than the younger ones and in this study there were no differences between boys and girls. History was superior in developing moral judgment than was a programme in environmental studies, though there was doubt whether this conclusion 'would apply to other integrated studies like social studies, where moral education might be more central' (Simon and Ward, 1972).

In part the tendency towards integrated studies in secondary schools – much work at the primary level is perforce of this nature – owes much to one reaction towards the growth of specialization. Since individuals are seen as so important they are to be seen as wholes, not as made up of intellectual sectors, each of which is treated by a specialist. Indeed, this 'artificial compartmentalization' has been seen by two radical critics of traditional schooling as 'militat(ing) against the application of comprehensive moral standards or the consideration of the larger social consequences of one's work' (Bowles and Gintis, 1976, p. 207). Thus, the boundaries between the subjects and between the bailiwicks of experts must be broken down so that the individual can exist again as a whole. But integrated curricula resulting from such ideas can be divided very broadly into two kinds, those whose basic rationale is seen as purely pedagogical and those which are founded on a radical political ideology.

An example of the former type is the Schools Council Humanities Project and of the latter the programmes emanating in the late-1960s from Goldsmith's College. The Humanities Project produced several packs of material on topics such as war and authority which were to be looked at with the aid of a number of the subjects usually known as the humanities. While the project's aims were perhaps not so conservative as those of Leavis there was a similarity to his approach to English teaching as it was hoped that what the classics had supposedly taught in the moral field would now be gained from a study of the modern humanities. In addition, there was the aim of teaching a rational approach to value judgments which would thereby be based on more than mere prejudice. The Goldsmith's curricula were far more radical in aim in that the style of pedagogy involved was probably seen as more important than the material used. Courses were based on enquiry, which would lead pupils beyond the present boundaries of existing subjects and, hence, to a questioning of the authority supporting such positions. Furthermore, much of the direction of courses would be negotiated between pupils and teachers so that a democratic way of relating to others, particularly to members of the older generation, would be learnt. Clearly this pedagogy was supposed to form a moral lesson in itself (Musgrave, 1972).

Attempts to evaluate such integrated programmes are rare. King has carried out a study of the movement of pupils from traditional and open primary schools to traditional and open secondary schools in Victoria. He found that where pupils move to styles of pedagogy of which they as yet have no experience, whether it be from traditional to open or from open to traditional, they suffer adverse effects. This tendency operates for measures of both academic progress and personal development so that it would appear that the moral curriculum involved in open teaching may under certain quite common circumstances not be learnt (King, 1974).

To sum up: clearly the academic curriculum can only be divorced from the moral curriculum in theory. In practice English and history have both been used, consciously and unconsciously, to teach moral lessons. There is evidence to show some success in this field, but little is known about what makes for success and how frequently it occurs. Integrated courses that contain elements of these subjects and of other humanities sometimes rely openly on the style of their pedagogy to achieve moral results. Their development, as has been the case for the separate subjects, has been closely related to social changes occurring largely outside the field of education itself.

Moral education

The drive towards social efficiency following the Boer War was not only directed towards improving physique, but also to producing adults who in some sense had tougher characters. Individual initiative, endurance, loyalty and a sense of service had social functions in strengthening the mother country and in maintaining the Empire. It is in this context that much of Kipling's writing after 1900 may be viewed. Sadler's two volumes (1908) indicate that there was at this time a strong demand for moral education. Indeed, much of this demand had been created by the Moral Instruction League, founded in 1897 and renamed the Moral Education League in 1909. This body's 'influence was at its height from 1902 to 1908' (Selleck, 1968, p. 312). Sadler himself divided the task in this whole field into two parts: 'Moral training aims at giving good habits; moral instruction at imparting moral ideas' (p. xxxix). The latter had by its nature to come from 'direct' methods, usually from teaching, whilst the former was imparted in all the various indirect ways that have so far been considered here. It is to what Sadler called 'moral instruction' that we shall now give our attention.

Several of those who contributed papers to Sadler's symposium commented on the importance of the fact that Morant's new Elementary Code of 1904 gave its blessing to moral instruction. In his Introduction to this Code he wrote, 'The purpose of the Public Elementary School is to form and strengthen the character and to develop the intelligence of the child entrusted to it'. This Introduction was included in subsequent revisions of the Code until the elementary school disappeared as a school type after the enactment of the 1944 Act. In the 1906 Code, and this too was welcomed by Sadler's contributors, an entry was included on 'Moral Instruction' under Article 2. This subject 'should form an important part of the curriculum in every elementary school. Such instruction may either (i) be incidental, occasional ..., or (ii) be given systematically and as a course of graduated instruction.' The instruction was to be directed towards a list of moral qualities such as has several times already been cited here.

By and large the instruction was occasional and incidental in the public schools and also in the state-provided schools, though in the latter there were perhaps more opportunities available in such academic subjects as hygiene and domestic science, whilst in the former the opportunities came more often in chapel or on the games field. However, the direct instruction given tended to be abstract in character; deductive in that principles were stated and had to be related to practice rather than the reverse process; passive, since instruction largely occurred in the classroom; irrational in the sense that morality was based on an authority whose power was not to be tested by reason; negative in that 'do not' was a more common prescription than 'thou shalt'; and, finally, conflict was largely ignored, since the overlapping moral interests of actors in the real world were forgotten (Bull, 1969, pp. 133–7).

Since around 1960, however, 'the new morality' has based itself on a different approach. Robinson has written: 'Of course, the inductive approach is more dangerous. The ends are not prescribed, the answers are not settled beforehand. But this is only to say that a real *decision* is involved in any responsible moral choice' (1964, p. 41; italics in original). This induction has to be applied to 'the nuclear moral experience consist(ing) of [a] mutuality of respect and freedom' (Loukes, 1975, p. 212). There is evidence both in the data concerning teenagers cited earlier in this book and in McPhail's work to support Loukes' view that the contemporary units of moral analysis consist of interpersonal behaviour. His respondents were quite clear that consideration for the needs, interests and feelings of others was the main focus of morality (1972, p. 47). He, therefore, concluded that curricula in the field of moral education should build on this.

The *Lifeline* material which emerged from the Schools Council project led by McPhail was based on this inductive approach and unlike traditional moral education was concrete, active, rational, positive and took note of conflict. The aim was no longer to teach a set of prescriptions, but to ensure that children knew how to cope with moral dilemmas. The American philosopher, Scheffler (1965), had differentiated between 'to know that' and 'to know how to'. This epistemological distinction was a crucial one in the philosophical justification of discovery methods in science education; it was now applied to moral education.

But serving teachers had varying ideas on how this moral competency might best be taught. There were some avant-garde programmes. Thus, in one London comprehensive school a fourth-form group had weekly sessions whose aim was 'to build a "good group", that is, one to which the members felt they belonged and could make what seemed a worthwhile contribution' (Clark, 1975). In such a programme the subjective criterion used and the emphasis on constructing a morality are both much at odds with traditional methods in moral education. However, it would seem that most teachers still see the use of contemporary versions of traditional curricular material as most suited to teaching moral education and in such terms it is that the *Lifeline* material may best be described.

The materials are aimed 'to help young people . . . in the 13–16 age range, adopt a considerate style of life'. There are three sets of material. The first is entitled, 'In other people's shoes', which 'deals with the difficulties that arise between individuals mainly in two-person situations'. Largely by role-playing the student is encouraged to be sensitive to others and to the consequences of his actions for others; he comes, it is hoped, 'to understand better what makes people tick'. The second set is called 'Proving the rule' and 'deals with the problems that arise for the individual in society'. The third set, 'What would you have done?' provides materials so that teenagers may look at 'moral-social problems in a world-wide context, and move(s) out from the more immediate situation of the other *Lifeline* material'. McPhail has said:

The aim of the series is to help boys and girls to develop a strong sense of identity and see themselves as people who have a contribution to make in their community, without at the same time telling them what kind of adults they ought to be or what system of values and beliefs they ought to have. (McPhail, 1972, p. 112)

There is no doubt that this material owes much to the spirit of 'the new morality', to its tolerance and rootedness in situations, and to its empiricism, especially interpreted in terms of the social sciences. We have already noted that McPhail has published evidence to show that this programme does change the behaviour of young people (pp. 17–18) and in a very honest way he raises the issue whether this is no more than a new and extremely subtle form of conditioning.

The new type of expert who develops curricular materials in moral education can easily become or be seen as a technologist of moral consent despite his disclaimer that choice has been handed to the pupil. Choice, it will be said, can be manipulated as so often is the case with subject choice when schools offer options to their pupils. Who are the moral experts? asks Miller (1975). It should be noted that moral experts are not necessarily seen by society as agents of respectability. Indeed, for their central definition of morality the experts developing the *Lifeline* material consulted as one of their agents of respectability the children on whose behalf they were using their professional expertise.

The philosopher Singer's view is that moral philosophers are likely to be more expert in this field than laymen in view of their specialized training, their understanding of moral concepts, and their full-time work on moral issues (Singer, 1972). Schutz might have felt that such experts would be blind to much, but undoubtedly their expertise should enable the delivery to teachers of well-designed materials. Yet materials are designed for a purpose. *Lifeline*'s purpose, as has just been indicated, was in great part decided by those who were to benefit from it, namely the pupils. They chose 'considerateness'. Yet this choice also might have been built into them socially.

This circularity in attempts to justify the aims of moral education may be avoided in three ways. Aims can be drawn from a revealed religion, though in this age few admit to religious belief – rather more have political beliefs which function as religious beliefs once did. Or philosophers may help us to specify aims, but so far they have not been able to do this, because of the philosophical gap associated with the naturalistic fallacy, that is the logical difficulties implicit in moving from what is to what ought to be. Or, finally, moral education must be related to the society in which the pupils concerned are to live. It is to problems of this nature amongst others that we shall turn in the last chapter.

Conclusion

Throughout the consideration in this chapter of the various elements of the moral curriculum the point has been made frequently that the relevant parts of the organization of the school or the relevant school subjects have changed and are changing in a way that has paralleled the social tendencies outlined in the previous chapter. Very rarely has a change taken place that can be seen as purely educational in its origin. The one possible exception cited here might be the influence on teaching methods of Scheffler's work in epistemology, but its application in the development of curricula in moral education again matched existing social tendencies. Indeed, without knowing much of the history of contemporary philosophy it would be hard to deny the possibility that Scheffler may himself have been encouraged to think the way in which he did by these very tendencies.

In brief, subjects have become less prescriptive, more tolerant of differences, more secular in spirit, less competitive and more open to the influence of the growth of the social sciences. Methods of organizing schools have also tended to change along similar dimensions in order to cope with the new ethos. What is in some doubt is how much new moral qualities are being taught and how much the old qualities are being taught in more cunning ways. However, in one respect so great has been the change that one part of the administrative framework for education, that concerning the production of agreed syllabuses in religious education, now probably constrains further development along the present lines. Certainly, it is true that no longer does 'the easy and ever-repeated reading' of the Bible make young people 'wise unto salvation' and 'refined beyond "the guess of folly"' – if it ever did.

6

Conclusion: the moral curriculum, society and change

> Le vice et le vertu sont des produits comme le vitriol et le sucre
>
> (Henri Taine, *Introduction to the History of English Literature*, 1863)

Thus far in this book we have focused on two levels of analysis in examining the relationships between morality and moral education. Firstly, at the interpersonal level, the process of moral choice amongst teenagers was examined. Such choices seem to be based largely on recipes or principles learnt in childhood in the family which are usually applied in a routine way. From time to time, however, some individual crisis drives a moral actor to reflection about what he ought to do. It is to these reflective moral decisions that we must look if we want to find the seeds of change in the moral codes of a society.

All moral decisions, routine or reflective, are taken in social situations, which may also be conceptualized as occurring against a backdrop of the social system. Our second level of analysis is related to the wider social system, but seen here in historical terms. Those with power in any society will have some conception of the code of morality which they aim to maintain. They, or agents acting on their behalf, will seek to transmit and support a code of respectability. There will be some continuity with the past in any society, though the rate of social change will govern how great this link will be. We have seen that in Britain, despite changes, there are many influences still at work that relate both to a code of morality upheld in the earlier years of this century and to the structure of power which was concerned to support it. The vocabularies of motive that those in schools try to impart are much constrained by the history of the educational system.

However, in Britain there has been a change in the balance of power between the social classes so that no longer is the upper middle class so nearly all-powerful. This new situation has allowed the possibility of more than one code of morality co-existing. At the turn of the century the schools were involved in attempting to impose a unitary code, deferential in its prescriptions for behaviour between ruler and ruled. Admittedly there were different versions for each class and ranges of tolerated behaviour within each version, but the code was seen by those running the schools as unitary. Since around 1960 much has altered. Now the moral code transmitted in the schools seems to be moving towards a self-chosen and egalitarian one. Hence, pluralism has become not just a possibility, but a reality.

The evidence presented so far has almost entirely been British. The first aim of this concluding chapter is, therefore, to extend the range of the analysis by citing some comparative data. This, secondly, will raise some theoretical issues that directly relate to the position of those with power over morals in any society. Finally, we must be concerned with implications which the whole analysis has for moral education in the schools.

Some comparative evidence

At the start of Chapter 2 the approach to moral education through comparing the social institutions of various societies was mentioned and apparently put on one side by the concentration on British evidence. In one sense intellectual legerdemain has been practised on the reader in that the historical analysis of Chapter 4 can be seen as a comparison of two somewhat different societies, namely Britain in 1900 and Britain in 1970. Something can be learnt from such 'close' comparisons, but 'distant' comparison between societies very different in nature can also add to our understanding. It is, therefore, proposed to cite some evidence, first, from anthropological sources and, second, concerning the

USSR. In the first case the societies concerned are very different, some purists might even say not comparable, to Britain and in the latter case, though the social structure is somewhat similar to that in Britain, the way in which political power is wielded is dissimilar.

Anthropological evidence

There is a Ugandan tribe, called the Ik, who live in the mountains on the Sudan border. The Ik were formerly a hunting people but in the fifties their hunting lands were converted by the government into a game reserve. The Ik refused to move elsewhere and as a result their way of life no longer matched their physical environment. In their fight for physical survival they evolved a code based upon the principle of 'devil take the hindmost'. As an example one may cite the incident observed by the anthropologist, Turnbull, who worked amongst the Ik, when halfmasticated food was removed from the mouth of an old, very weak, dying person and eaten by a younger and fitter man. Qualities that we see as primary virtues are seen by the Ik as 'not inherent in humanity at all, ... not a necessary part of human nature'.

> The Ik have successfully abandoned useless appendages, those basic qualities such as family, cooperative sociality, belief, love, hope and so forth, for the very good reason that in their context these militated against survival. (Turnbull, 1974, pp. 238–9)

Each member of the Ik suffered a profound crisis because of which his whole way of life came into question. A new code of morality evolved to meet the new environment. No longer did the Ik treat persons as persons in the way we know. They learned by example when young that this would not lead to survival. The locus of any authority in this tribe was hard to pinpoint, but there was a diffused sense of deference to certain persons who were seen as cleverer in that environment and of loyalty to certain sacred objects. Yet the individual and his physical needs were central to the way of life.

This code of morality – to us, maybe, of immorality – may be compared with that of the Gahuku-Gama, a pastoral tribe in the Eastern Highland of Papua New Guinea. Amongst them 'stated as sharply as possible, moral obligations are primarily contingent on the social position of individuals' (Read, 1955, p. 199). Thus,

116

for example, the Gahuku-Gama do not judge the actions of non-members of their society in the same way as those who are members. Indeed, if questioned concerning the behaviour of 'foreigners' they usually answer, 'I don't understand'. For us who operate under moral codes associated with the Judaeo-Christian tradition the source of authority is seen as outside the particular system of social relationships in which we are involved. Our morality is, in a word, universalistic, but to the Gahuku-Gama 'men are not primarily persons, in the moral sense, but social individuals' (p. 206).

In each of these cases a morality has been constructed which enables its holders to live in their environment. In one crucial respect the codes vary from ours; the considerateness of others that is based on a universal respect for any individual as a person is totally absent for the Ik and absent for the Gahuku-Gama in that they do not judge *all* humans by the same criteria. This raises a problem in relation to Wilson's analysis cited earlier (1973) in which he attempts to evolve a universally applicable framework of moral thinking. One of the elements suggested by him was called PHIL and this concerned understanding persons as persons. It may be that both the Ik and the Gahuku-Gama do consider individuals in their moral thinking, but they do so in a totally different way from that used by us, namely in an indivi-dualistic manner amongst the Ik and in a socially determined way amongst the Gahuku-Gama.

The USSR

In the years immediately after the Russian Revolution of 1917 disorderliness amongst youth was a great problem in the USSR. The gangs of homeless young persons who roamed the country-side and cities living in a very anti-social manner were called *Besprizorniki* and in 1922 on one calculation numbered seven millions (Bowen, 1965, p. 47). Like the Ik, but as gangs not in-dividuals, they lived for themselves and, hence, acted in a way that was opposed to the new socialist concept of each individual work-ing co-operatively for the greater good of the society. An obscure young teacher in the Ukraine, A. S. Makarenko, believed that he could develop a pedagogy that would deal with this problem. He established a colony of a small number of young persons who learned to live and work together largely as a result of the very strong group sanctions that Makarenko managed to create. He successively organized three such colonies and became famous because of his success. He published his experiences and methods mainly in the form of novels which are still one basis of pedagogy in the USSR. Makarenko never deviated from

> his belief in the necessity for first structuring the group ... To that had to be added the principle of developing and maintaining a strong in-group cohesion with an almost ruthless regard for trespassers of social norms. With such an emphasis on the power of environmental moulding, the individual past of each person mattered little ... the collective had to have a motivation that came as an external challenge, symbolized by the concept of Stakhanovism. (p. 166)

The sanctions of peers were used to support the moral code laid down by those in power. Makarenko made sure that the individualistic delinquents who came to his colonies worked and learned in a co-operative way that would ultimately help the achievement of a socialist society as he defined it.

More recent research in the USSR has shown that Makarenko's pedagogy still underlies the moral curriculum of the schools (Bronfenbrenner, 1971). The society is given priority over the individual so that discipline is achieved through collective means. The school is organized so that class committees and even subgroups, called 'links', within classes deal with those who fail to live up to the norms, moral or otherwise, laid down for its pupils. Competition is not between individuals, but is between groups within the school or between schools. So strong is the organization of the school that 'Soviet children are much less willing to engage in antisocial behaviour than their age mates in' the USA, England or Germany (p. 78). In specific detail teachers aim through their teaching and through the organization of the school to develop, in the words of an influential Russian writer, 'relations of mutual dependence, mutual responsibility, mutual control, subordination and commanding, and intolerance to persons interfering with common tasks' (p. 87). Though there is some slippage, by and large the methods used seem to succeed so that 'the children appear to be obedient; they are also self-disciplined, at least at the level of the collective' (p. 80).

In this case those in charge of the educational system of one country gradually evolved a pedagogical system that matched their political ideology and used it as an instrument of change to achieve a new morality in its young persons. Ultimately, the same pedagogy has been used to maintain the code of morality that has now apparently been largely accepted in the USSR. There remain some problems of delinquency and of excluding unwelcome influences from outside the USSR, but basically it is still possible to make the point that Peters did and that was quoted in Chapter 2, namely that in the moral code that has been constructed by those in power in the USSR no one is expected to reach Kohlberg's sixth and final stage of moral autonomy. Once again a principle for which universal application has been claimed is challenged by sociological analysis.

Agents of respectability

In each of the comparisons that have been made with Britain there is a different set of agents of respectability at work. Admittedly in Britain the situation is confused and must be so if a plurality of codes is to exist. Parents are clearly very important, but teachers do not seem to be seen as strong influences in the field of morality, certainly at secondary school level. Peers are, however, influential by this age, but as courts of appeal or for advice rather than as a structured part of the moral curriculum. In the USSR parents work closely with teachers who structure schools at every stage to gain the support of peers to inculcate a social, not an individual morality. The division between moral transgression and mental health is much more certain in the situation of the USSR where political power is wielded very firmly in support of the official ideology. There is not the same need for the creation of an army of para-professionals or counsellors whose training and practice owes much to medical modes of thought to assist those under strain to cope with the problems of living as there is in a society where much leisure, general wealth and the ruling ideology enable a wide range of choice to be made.

Amongst the Ik and the Gahuku-Gama there are no powerful specialized agents to do the society's respectability work. The authority that supports the moral code is diffused throughout the society. In such small societies reports concerning moral transgression quickly reach the ears of someone with some power over the young, be it a parent, a relative or a tribal elder, so that sanctions can be brought to bear if need be. For the Ik the need is rare because to ensure survival almost any action is allowable, but at least in childhood the only way to survive is to imitate the behaviour of 'respected' adults.

The comparative evidence cited here reinforces the point made earlier that moral codes are social creations that are man-made and hence at least in theory can be changed. In addition, the comparison between the anthropological data, particularly relating to the Ik, and that for Britain and the USSR raises the question of whether or not authority, as Durkheim posited, is necessary to ensure a society's code of morality.

Social norms and power

The concept of 'norms' was mentioned in Chapter 2, but not as a basis for any theoretical argument. Here, following the argument of Dahrendorf in his inaugural lecture (1968), this concept will be used to develop an analysis that supports the empirical position that has apparently been reached concerning the important position of authority in relation to the moral code of any society.

Dahrendorf was concerned with the origins of material inequality in societies. However, his analysis can be applied in the context where the concern is with the unequal distribution of power. He argued that any human society is inescapably regulated by established expectations of behaviour. If this were not so we could hardly give it the name of a society. In their abstract form such expectations are conceptualized by members as norms, many of which are moral in nature in that they constrain how members treat each other. Thus, every society is in a sense a moral community in that actions are governed by generally held norms. In this situation someone must have the power of 'sanctioning behaviour according to whether it does or does not conform to established norms' (p. 167). If deviants escaped punishment social norms would be challenged successfully so that the possibility will arise of establishing a new and changed set of norms. Dahrendorf summed up his position in these terse words: 'Society *means* that norms regulate human conduct; this regulation is guaranteed by the incentive or threat of sanctions; the possibility of imposing sanctions is the abstract core of all power' (p. 173).

This view of any society as operating under some more or less well-agreed set of norms, one important part of which is its moral code and with sanctions in the hands of those who hold power, fits well with what we have seen to be the case historically in Britain and now in the USSR. In the latter country a strongly entrenched political party controls the schools and ensures that the morality that it supports is taught both directly and as a result of the way the schools are organized. In Britain the situation could be seen in a similar way at the start of the century, but is now rather more fluid. Yet there is still a very complex administrative mechanism that includes schools and the counselling professions whose aim is to ensure that despite the plurality of codes now permissible those who test too far the boundaries of moral normality will be brought to book in as kind a way as possible.

Very often it is those who press against the limits of present moral norms who in fact establish the exact boundaries of permissible behaviour (Erikson, 1962). But it is the presence of norms, however constructed, that in Dahrendorf's sense defines the existence of a society. However, there is an additional point that can be made. As a result of the analysis in Chapter 3 we can see that it is the activity of moral entrepeneurs, if not successfully sanctioned, that can lead to changes in moral codes. The advocates of 'the new morality' in the sixties were not so checked and founded a new orthodoxy, which permits a wide range of behaviour and even of plural moralities. Yet, if no boundaries to the possible plurality of codes is set, there is the possibility either of moral chaos or of the representatives of some new orthodoxy grasping power in order to transmit their preferred set of moral norms. What is being said is that beyond some point plurality can become unstable. The Ik are possibly in such a position of instability as, indeed, may any society be in which authority is very diffused. There may be no power in these social systems strong enough to ensure that the presently agreed norms are adhered to.

This sociological analysis, therefore, supports a conclusion that moral codes must be seen as man-made and as specific to one social system, changing through conflict, but sanctioned by those holding or seeking power. This is a very different picture from that drawn by some philosophers who write in terms of universals and of justification through clarification of the concepts used and through logical analysis. However, at least one philosopher of education has recently adopted a position that is parallel to that reached here. After pointing out that there is no possibility of reaching a set of prescriptions for action by employing formal moral reasoning Watt (1976) has concluded that at some point someone must add such a substantive rule as 'don't hurt others' (p. 14). He wishes to see such recipes, or the principles that underlie them, not as 'beliefs' but as 'policies'. They then can be examined in a community, rather than an individual setting and rational argument about them becomes possible. 'Policies must be vindicated first and foremost as means to *communal* ends' (p. 25).

The man-made nature of morality has also been argued by psychologists. Thus, Bull has pointed out that feral children have no morality, but have to learn one when they enter a society (1969, pp. 13–14). The additional sociological point being made here is that the norms of morality are an inevitable part of any stable, or at least slowly changing, society, though the code that the rulers of a society try to enforce or allow to exist will vary according to their beliefs, the culture and the history of that society.

There is a further point that must be made. The instability of some societies has been mentioned. In the case of the Ik power is so diffuse that no truly social code, it seems, is enforced. Some persons are critical of the present moral position in Britain because they see a somewhat similar situation here. Moral power has become so diffuse that no one code, particularly in relation to secondary virtues, need necessarily be followed. Ultimately, they feel either moral anarchy will ensue, or some new group will take power and, as was the case after 1917 in the USSR, impose their version of morality. However, Stanley has gone further than this by indicating that moral instability is implicit in all societies however stable they may appear at any one particular time. Since society may be conceptualized as 'a mosaic of meanings' there is always the possibility that a meaning may 'suggest to people, by means of implications, possibilities for operational concretizations *other than* those achieved up to a given point of time ... All meanings are, therefore, open pointing in some direction of the "not yet" ' (Stanley, 1973, p. 440).

In real terms, following Stanley's analysis, we may suddenly realize ourselves in some sense to be deprived and say 'it isn't fair' so that we may be driven to action that could lead to an attempt to renegotiate the current moral code. Any individual may be involved in such a challenge though in this connection we tend to think of the great men in history – Rousseau for example – who have written suggesting new moral codes. However, great men are only sociologically interesting if their actions bring into being new norms which cause different behaviour in others. Such an outcome will depend not only on the personality of the individual who makes such a reflective moral decision, but on the nature of the social structure within which he acts.

In terms of the earlier mentioned concepts, pioneered by Mary Douglas (1970), the strength of 'group' and 'grid' are crucial. Where groups have strong boundaries and where the matrix of roles is tightly drawn, as in both cases is truer of the USSR than of Britain, there will be a tendency for social control mechanisms to be brought to bear actively against those who break the norms. Furthermore, the range of tolerated behaviour within any one norm will be narrow. Where 'group' and 'grid' are weaker, as in Britain in comparison with the USSR, the opposite will be the case and the changing of norms will be much more of a possibility. The important point upon which we must focus here is the particular structural characteristics which govern this process. The key seems to be the nature of the interaction between moral actors and agents of respectability. The more simple is the structure of the society or the more direct are the relationships between actors and those with power over moral actions, even though such relationships may be diffused as amongst the Ik or the Gahuku-Gama, the easier is feed-back concerning acts seen as immoral and, hence, the more difficult is moral change.

If a society is to remain a whole, there must be somewhere, as Dahrendorf has recently shown and as Durkheim earlier indicated, a source of moral authority. If a group with power can assert some 'policy' concerning the primary and secondary virtues that it wants to be seen as normative for that society then change will be checked. Karl Mannheim (1940, pp. 82–3) was interested in the position of authority in democratic societies. He distinguished six types of élite, one of which he named 'the moral élite'. This concept can be seen as another formulation to cover what have here been termed 'agents of respectability'. Mannheim went on to consider the changes then at work in democratic societies which he considered were destroying the old élites. In some respects his analysis paralleled that of Chapter 4 since he emphasized the increasing numbers of those claiming élite status and the way in which this process destroyed the exclusiveness of such groups. He also commented on the conflict involved in such processes and on the alternative solutions through autocracy or democracy. He was keen to organize society in such a way that some type of democracy was preserved. The problem is that, as already indicated, in all probability no single solution can guarantee permanent stability.

Thus, when any change in morality does occur the new moral code must never be seen as a return to an equilibrium, but as the result of a conflict between those with power and, hence, as a position which is ultimately as precarious as any other such position has always been in the past and always will be in the future. Furthermore, one can only speculate who will hold power in, for example, Britain in the future; there are as yet no sociological laws that allow such a prediction. If we continue to think in terms of social class, we may ask whether there are signs of a new class arising to claim power. There are two contemporary groups who hold codes somewhat different from those outlined in Chapter 4 and who are also opposed to each other. Both may be described as members of 'the intelligentsia', though one of these new groups acts critically within society whilst the other does so from outside the existing system (Hawthorn, 1976). The first is made up of the 'technocrats' – men and women who have often arrived at their present position of power because of what is seen as their merit and who also see their aim to be to ensure that our present social system is operated as efficiently and fairly – by their criteria – as possible. The second group consists of those who have 'dropped out' of society in one way or another. For them the central aim of the technocrats is wrong, because to run the system efficiently means nothing to those who believe it to be a system that is itself morally wrong. Each group perforce supports a different moral code, almost diametrically opposed to that of the other. The former is competitive and universalistic – almost a bureaucratic morality; the latter is individualistic and situational, and may with interest be compared to the morality of the Gahuku-Gama. In the long revolution of British history one would predict that some compromise will evolve in which the former will have more influence upon the old centres of power, but in which some of the radical implications of the latter are not forgotten. Or is one here merely rationalizing one's own desires?

Moral education

In the USSR a particular moral code is openly transmitted in schools in which a method of organization is specifically structured to support the desired lessons, but in Britain the process is much less planned. Again, in the USSR there is continuity between school and adult life. The experiences gained by the young at school from the formal lessons taught and from the ways in which the school is organized closely parallel the experiences that will be undergone in factory and trade union when adult. The norms of the wider society are clearly represented in the organizations available to citizens so that the social structure is planned to uphold the version of respectability considered necessary by those with power in Soviet society. In Britain the life cycle is much less planned. Indeed, Baumann has written of the movement through adolescence in Western societies as both 'a transition from nowhere' and 'a transition to nowhere' (1967, p. 328). Adolescence is seen as an experimental period between schooldays and adulthood, a time during which the moral codes learned in childhood may be reconsidered and retained or not. Such a position would be supported by some of the evidence cited earlier from the interviews with teenagers.

During this same period, however, the pressures, for example, from advertising and the commercialized leisure industries are today very powerful so that a firm sense of identity is needed at the very moment when a moratorium upon present identity is thrust upon the adolescents concerned. In these circumstances it is not surprising that in Britain problems of mental health, an area defined by most persons as well within medical competence, have become very central to adolescence. Yet in this same social context we may well ask what can those involved in moral education in the schools do for their pupils?

This analysis began from the act of moral choice, and a sociological description of moral decisions has been given. Moral education must aim to influence such decisions. It must, therefore, take account of the way in which these choices seem to be made. Attention must be given to the knowledge needed, the relevant structures to be used, the skills necessary for interpreting the thoughts, feelings and actions of others involved, and to the process of weighting used by moral actors as they balance the three elements already mentioned. Teaching about these four elements and practice in using them must be built into programmes of moral education. In the last chapter we have seen that contemporary curricular development has paid some attention to the first three elements, but that so far little or no conscious effort is apparently being made to teach children of any age about the fourth element, namely the judgmental or weighting process, which is ultimately crucial in any moral decisions.

Though attention has been given to the first three elements in moral decisions there are, nevertheless, still some important problems to which further consideration could be given. These specifically relate to curricular pacing. At what age should particular aspects of these elements be introduced? Many decisions about the timing of the introduction of parts of the academic curriculum depend upon socially determined decisions and the same seems true of the moral curriculum. Why, for example, has sex education been excluded for so long from many primary schools? And, if it is to be introduced at this stage, in what form should this be done? Furthermore, since the majority of pupils leave school by sixteen, what differences should there be in the moral curriculum for those who leave at the minimum legal age and for those whose 'privileged puberty' (Rosenmayr, 1968, p. 311) extends to eighteen or even twenty-one?

Not all the present problems of the moral curriculum relate to its content or pacing. Indeed, there is a prior problem that concerns school structure, namely, what should be the status of the teacher? At present the teacher does not appear to be an accepted agent of respectability for most adolescents. This was clear from the evidence presented in Chapter 3. As early as 1962 Wright had found a similar situation in a sample $(N=105)$ of fourth-year pupils of a secondary modern school in a small, semi-industrial town in Oxfordshire. These teenagers were 'a good deal less identified with their teachers than [with] their parents', but

> Insofar as pupils [did] identify with teachers, [this was] restricted to those aspects of personality which relate to academic achievement. They admire their cleverness and knowledge. But they do not seem to value them highly as persons. It is precisely these aspects of the teacher's personality which makes him human that are rated unfavourably. Teachers are not happy, easy going, trustful and popular. (1962, pp. 231–2)

We have seen that teenagers claim to want some help from schools in moral matters, but clearly, if they are to see teachers as agents of moral as well as academic respectability, teachers must recognize their present weak position as moral authorities. In such a situation to try to impose their views from a position of authority spells almost certain failure, whereas to teach by example or through reasoned discussions stands a greater chance of success.

That a teacher should be a moral example implies commitment to some position. Such commitment should result in behaviour of a certain moral nature. A common criticism of the upper middle class around 1900 was that they did not live up to their moral code. Teachers must do as they say if they wish to teach successfully. Today the difficulty is that the chance to choose has so high a priority that the teaching of any one moral code has become hard to justify. The worst situation in the eyes of many contemporary adolescents is one in which choice is apparently allowed, but in which in reality no choice is available and pupils are conditioned into one specific set of choices.

Apart from the sociological argument that agents of respectability, amongst whom in most contemporary societies teachers are supposedly numbered, must work from authority to preserve an explained and rational code of morality it can be argued philosophically that a morally neutral teacher is an impossibility. 'Someone who really takes a morally neutral stance is not only unable to *solve* any moral dilemmas, he is unable to *notice* any' (Watt, 1976, p. 80).

The commitment of a teacher to a moral stance, however, raises one major problem. The teacher may be opposed to the moral code that the school itself is trying to pass on to its pupils. Such disagreement may well be supportable if it involves only one teacher and relates to the secondary virtues. Certainly there will be difficulties where the difference concerns the primary virtues or where parents are not tolerant of the situation. Because nearly all persons see themselves as moral experts where only teachers are academic experts there is every chance that, where one or more teachers try to teach a moral code that differs from that of the majority of the local inhabitants, parents will object. They may well use whatever power they have, through, for example, participation in school governance, to prevent teachers, seen by them as deviant, from pursuing the aims of teaching their children a changed moral code. In such circumstances these teachers can be seen as testing the boundaries of respectability and in the conflict that can ensue they may well lose their case.

Conclusion

The analysis of this book will be concluded by presenting six summary statements:

(1) In making moral decisions actors do have some room for manoeuvre in constructing their own codes of morality, but the range of tolerated behaviour towards others varies from one

society to another. However, when a very wide range is allowed or where a plurality of codes is permissible, a more than usually unstable position exists. This tends to lead to a new situation in which a fresh range of permissible moral action may come into existence.

(2) Change is always near. Morality is as precarious in a society as it is in a school. The direction of change is hard to predict and need not, as was believed by many in the nineteenth century, be in an increasingly liberal direction. Both the Ik and the USSR have moved in the opposite direction in the eyes of many contemporary observers.

(3) Moral codes are social constructions, born in the redefinition of meanings by individuals, and justified by members of societies according to or within the ideologies of groups with power, though this does not mean that an existing group may not be taken over by, or take over, a new morality, as was the case with Christianity in the Roman Empire.

(4) There are agents of respectability in any society who enforce the code of that society and a major part of what is seen by many as our present moral problem can be analysed in terms of the weakness and uncertain location of these agents of respectability in society today. In addition, these agents of respectability can be found in unexpected parts of the social system, as has been the case with the influence of medical men on moral education in British schools. Furthermore, the influence of any one agent, or set of agents, of respectability may continue through time, but be exercised over different parts of a moral code. Again, since 1900 doctors in Britain have shown this to be true in that they have switched their connection with schools from an emphasis on 'good habits' to a stress on mental health.

(5) The content of the moral curriculum, its pedagogy and pacing, the academic subjects to be involved and the school organization needed are all very clearly related to the total social structure within which any school is set, though lags may occur so that the school is teaching a moral curriculum attuned to the past rather than to the present. Very rarely does a school attempt to change the moral code of a society, but where it does there is the constant danger that it will be constrained either by those in power or by the parents of its pupils. Certainly in the past the constraint has rarely come from the pupils themselves.

(6) The task of the moral critic in education, as in any other part of society, is a hard one. He must challenge the contemporary

128

code of respectability and sustain this challenge against society's agents of respectability so as to convert his ideals into the practical details of a moral curriculum that is strange to his society. Thomas Arnold and Makarenko each did this, as did some unsung members of the Ik. Matthew Arnold tried to do the same with only partial success. Alec Waugh completely failed. As *The Little Red School Book* said in its last paragraph, presumably with the aim of stirring those of school age to try to achieve moral change: 'Work for change always starts with you. The struggle is carried on by many different people in many different places. But it's the same struggle: (Hansen and Jensen, 1971, p. 207)

Social constraints are very strong and must never be overlooked, but *individuals* do sustain or change societies by their decisions. Because of the precarious nature of current moral meaning there will always be a tension between contemporary morality and what a few feel ought to be. There will, therefore, also always be problems of intense human concern in the field of moral education. The analysis of this book is aimed to provide some ways of thinking about these problems, though the very nature of human beings precludes any final solution.

References and
name index

The numbers in italics after each reference refer to page numbers within this book.

Armytage, W. H. G. (1975) Psycho-analysis and teacher education, I and II. *British Journal of Teacher Education 1(2)*: 227–36 and *1(3)*: 317–34. *80*

Baier, K. (1971) Ethical pluralism and moral education. In C. M. Beck, B. S. Crittenden and E. V. Sullivan (eds) *Moral Education*. Toronto: Toronto University Press. *21*

Ball, D. W. (1972) The problematics of respectability. In J. D. Douglas (ed.) *Deviance and Respectability*. New York: Basic Books. *25, 28*

Bamford, T. W. (1967) *Rise of the Public Schools*. London: Nelson. *64*

Bantock, G. H. (1967) *Education, Culture and the Emotions*. London: Faber & Faber. *86*

Barnes, S. B. (1969) Paradigms – Scientific and Social. *Man 4(1)*: 94–102. *31*

Baumann, Z. (1967) Some problems in contemporary education. *International Social Science Journal 19(3)*: 325–37. *125*

Bellah, R. N. (1973) Introduction. In *Emile Durkheim: On Morality and Society*. Chicago: University of Chicago Press. *18*

Bennett, N. (1976) *Teaching Styles and Pupil Progress*. London: Open Books. *54*

Berger P. L. and Luckmann T. (1967) *The Social Construction of Reality*. London: Allen Lane. *24*

Bibby, C. (1951) *Health Education: a guide to principles and practices*. London: Heinemann. *103*

Boltanski, L. (1969) *Prime education et morale de classe*. Paris: Editions de Minuit. *61*

Bowen, J. (1965) *Soviet Education: Anton Makarenko and the Years of Experiment*. Madison: University of Wisconsin Press. *117*

Bowlby, J. (1953) *Child Care and the Growth of Love*. London: Harmondsworth. *80*

Bowles, S. and Gintis, H. (1976) *Schooling in Capitalist America*. London: Routledge & Kegan Paul. *108*

Bronfenbrenner, U. (1971) *Two Worlds of Childhood*. London: Allen & Unwin. *118*

Bull, N. J. (1969) *Moral Education*. London: Routledge & Kegan Paul. *52, 110, 122*

Cahiers Internationaux de Sociologie (1964) Bibliographie de la Sociologie de la Vie Morale *36(1)*: 113–84. *16*

The Cambridgeshire Syllabus of Religious Teaching for Schools (1924, 1929, 1939, 1940 and 1949). Cambridge: Cambridge University Press. *96, 97*

Cannon, C. (1964) The influence of religion on educational policy since 1902. *British Journal of Educational Studies* 12(2): 143–60. *75*

Carpenter, P. (ed.) (1966) *Challenge*. London: Ward Lock. *96*

Carstairs, G. M. (1963) *This Island Now*. London: Hogarth Press. *77*

Carter, M. P. (1962) *Home, School and Work*. Oxford: Pergamon. *52*

Children and their Primary Schools (1967), Vols I and II. London: HMSO. *78*

Clark, D. B. (1975) Group work with early school leavers. *Journal of Curriculum Studies* 7(1): 42–54. *111*

Cohen, P. S. (1968) *Modern Social Theory*. London: Heinemann. *17*

Dahrendorf, R. (1968) *On the Origin of Inequality among Men* in *Essays in the Theory of Society*. London: Routledge & Kegan Paul, 151–78. *120*

Dingwall, R. (1977) Collectivism, regionalism and feminism: health visiting and British social policy, 1859–1975. *Journal of Social Policy* (forthcoming). *71*

Douglas, J. D. (1970) Deviance and respectability: the social construction of moral meanings. In J. D. Douglas (ed.) *Deviance and Respectability*. New York: Basic Books, 3–30. *29*

Douglas, M. (1970) *Natural Symbols*. London: Barrie & Rockcliffe. *26, 123*

Dukes, C. (1905) *Health at School considered in its Mental, Moral and Physical Aspects*. (4th edn) London: Rivington. *61, 63, 64*

Durkheim, E. (1961) *Moral Education*. New York: Free Press. *18, 22, 23, 26, 27, 78*

Emmet, D. (1966) *Rules, Roles and Relations*. London: Macmillan. *20*

Eppel, E. M. and E. (1966) *Adolescents and Morality*. London: Routledge & Kegan Paul. *20, 33, 44ff, 51*

Erikson, K. T. (1962) Notes on the sociology of deviance. *Social Problems 9(4)*: 307–14. *121*

Fitzgerald, R. T., Musgrave, P. W. and Pettit, D. W. (1976) *Participation in Schools?* Melbourne: Australian Council of Educational Research. *52, 55*

Fogelman, K. (ed.) (1976) *Britain's Sixteen-Year-Olds*. London: National Children's Bureau. *83*

Garfinkel, H. (1967) *Studies in Ethnomethodology*. Englewood Cliffs: Prentice-Hall. *34, 37*

Gerth, H. and Mills, C. W. (1954) *Character and Social Structure*. London: Routledge & Kegan Paul. *34, 59*

Gilbert, B. G. (1966) *The Evolution of National Insurance in Great Britain*. London: Michael Joseph. *70, 72*

Ginsberg, M. (1947) Moral progress in *Essays in Sociology and Social Progress, Vol. II*. London: Heinemann, 293–324. *17*

Goffman, E. (1952) On cooling the mark out; some aspects of adaption to failure. *Psychiatry 15(4)*: 451–63. *26*

Gosden, P. H. J. (1969) *How They Were Taught*. Oxford: Blackwell. *68*

Grace G. R. (1972) *Role Conflict and the Teacher*. London: Routledge & Kegan Paul. *53, 54*

Gurwitch, E. (1943) Is moral philosophy a normative theory? *Journal of Philosophy 40(6)*: 141–8. *17*

Halmos, P. (1965) *The Faith of the Counsellors*. London: Constable. *80, 85, 86*

Halmos, P. (1970) *The Personal Service Society*. London: Constable. *75, 80*

Hansen, I. V. (1974) A sense of community: the English public school sixth former. In S. Murray-Smith (ed.) *Melbourne Studies in Education, 1974.* Melbourne: Melbourne University Press. *90*

Hansen, S. and Jensen J. (1971) *The Little Red School Book.* London: Stage 1. *78, 94, 129*

Harding, D. W. (1953) *Social Psychology and Individual Values.* London: Hutchinson. *20*

Hare, R. M. (1952) *The Language of Morals.* Oxford: Oxford University Press. *21*

Hawthorn, G. (1976) The new intelligentsia in Britain. *New Society* 28 October: 183–6. *124*

Haystead, J. (1971) Social structure, awareness contexts and processes of choice. *Sociological Review 19(1)*: 79–94. *24, 37*

Hemming, J. (1963) Moral education in chaos. *New Society* 5 September. *79*

Highfield, M. E. and Pinsent, A. (1954) *A Survey of Rewards and Punishments in Schools,* London: Newnes. *91*

Hobhouse, L. T. (1906) *Morals in Evolution.* London: Chapman & Hall. *17*

Hull, J. M. (1975) Agreed syllabuses, past, present and future. In N. Smart and D. Horder (eds) *New Movements in Religious Education.* London: Temple Smith, 98–120. *96*

Humphreys, E. B. B. (1951) Home helps and health education. *Health Education Journal 9 (3):* 128–30. *71*

Kamm, J. (1965) *Hope Deferred.* London: Methuen. *62, 66*

Kay, J. (1975) Theory and management in health education. *Health Education Journal 34(3)*: 88–96. *85*

Kay, W. (1975) *Moral Education.* London: Allen and Unwin. *13, 19*

Kincaid, J. C. (1973) *Poverty and Equality in Britain.* Harmondsworth: Penguin. *72*

King, R. A. (1969) *Values and Involvement in a Grammar School.* London: Routledge & Kegan Paul. *92*

King, R. C. (1974) Innovation in the curriculum: a case study of open education. In P. W. Musgrave (ed.) *Contemporary Studies in the Curriculum.* Sydney: Angus & Robertson. *109*

Kohlberg, L. (1971) Stages of moral development as a basis for moral education. In E. M. Beck, B. S. Crittenden and E. V. Sullivan (eds) *Moral Education.* Toronto: University of Toronto Press, 24–84. *26*

Laing, R. D. (1960) *The Divided Self.* London: Tavistock. *82*

Laing, R. D. and Esterson, A. (1964) *Sanity, Madness and the Family*. London: Tavistock. *82*

Larson, L. E. (1972) The influence of parents and peers during adolescence: the situation hypothesis revisited. *Journal of Marriage and the Family 34(1)*: 67–74. *54*

Leavis, F. R. and Thompson, D. (1933) *Culture and Environment: The Training of Critical Awareness*. London: Chatto. *106*

Loubser, J. J. (1971) The contribution of schools to moral development: a working paper in the theory of action. In C. M. Beck, B. S. Crittenden and E. V. Sullivan (eds) *Moral Education*. Toronto: Toronto University Press, 147–77. *19*

Loukes, H. (1957) Pluralist education. In M. Taylor (ed.) *Progress and Problems in Moral Education*. Slough: National Foundation for Educational Research, 206–14. *110*

Mack, E. C. (1941) *Public Schools and British Opinion Since 1800*. London: Methuen. *63, 64*

Mannheim, K. (1940). *Man and Society in an Age of Reconstruction*. London: Routledge & Kegan Paul. *123*

McIntosh, P. C. (1968) *Physical Education in England since 1800* (2nd edn). London: Bell. *99, 100, 101*

McIntyre, A. C. (1967a) *A Short History of Ethics*. London: Routledge & Kegan Paul. *20*

McIntyre, A. C. (1967b) *Secularization and Moral Change*. London: Oxford University Press. *73, 79, 98*

McIntyre, A. C. (1971) What morality is not. In *Against the Self-Images of the Age*. London: Duckworth. *32*

McPhail, P., Ungoed-Thomas, J. R. and Chapman, H. (1972) *Moral Education in the Secondary School*. London: Longmans. *20, 43, 52, 53, 85, 98, 111, 112*

Mangan, J. A. (1975) Play up and play the game: Victorian and Edwardian public school vocabularies of motive. *Britsih Journal of Educational Studies 23(3)*: 324–35. *62*

Mathieson, M. (1975) *The Preachers of Culture*. London: Allen and Unwin. *105*

May, P. R. (1968) (1969) Attitudes of County Durham teachers to religious and moral education: Parts I and II. *Durham Research Review 5(21)*: 285–94 and *5(22)*: 351–7. *75, 83*

May, P. R. and Johnson, O. R. (1967) Parental attitudes to religious education in state schools. *Durham Research Review 5(18)*: 127–38. *79*

Merton, R. W. (1957) Social structure and anomie. In *Social Theory and Social Structure*. Glencoe: Free Press, 131–60. *28*

134

Miller, P. (1975) Who are the moral experts? *Journal of Moral Education* 5(*1*): 3–12. *112*

Miller, T. W. G. (1961) *Values in the Comprehensive School.* Edinburgh: Scottish Council for Research in Education. *93*

Moral & Religious Education in Scottish Schools (1972). Edinburgh: Her Majesty's Stationery Office. *53, 54, 55, 97, 104*

Morant, R. W. (1971) Some recent patterns of health education at the secondary level. *Health Education Journal* 30(2): 52–8. *103*

Mueller-Deham, A. (1944) The sociological foundations of ethics. *Ethics* 55(*1*): 9–27. *19, 22*

Musgrave, P. W. (1972) Two contemporary curricular ideologies. In R. J. W. Selleck (ed.) *Melbourne Studies in Education, 1972.* Melbourne: Melbourne University Press. *108*

Musgrave, P. W. (1973a) *Knowledge, Curriculum and Change.* Melbourne: Melbourne U.P. and London: Angus and Robertson. *13*

Musgrave, P. W. (1973b) 'Scrutiny' and education. *British Journal of Educational Studies* 21(3): 253–76. *106*

Musgrave, P. W. (1975) The place of social work in schools. *Journal of Community Studies* 10(*1*): 50–7. *75, 94*

Musgrave, P. W. (1976) Sociology and moral education: new directions. *Journal of Moral Education* 6(*1*): 14–21. *7*

Musgrave, P. W. (1977a) Corporal punishment in some English elementary schools, 1900–1939. *Research in Education* (forthcoming). *69, 84, 91*

Musgrave, P. W. (1977b) Moral decisions of some teenagers: a sociological account. *Cambridge Institute of Education Journal* (forthcoming). *7*

Musgrave, P. W. (1977c) Morality and the medical department: 1907–1974. *British Journal of Educational Studies* (forthcoming). *61, 70, 101, 102, 104*

Musgrove, F. and Taylor, P. H. (1969) *Society and the teacher's role.* London: Routledge & Kegan Paul. *53, 55*

Norwood, C. (1929) *The English Tradition in Education.* London: John Murray. *62*

Orr, K. (1963) Moral training in the boy scout movement. In E. L. French (ed.) *Melbourne Studies in Education, 1963.* Melbourne: Melbourne University Press. *95*

Ossowska, M. (1971) *Social Determinants of Moral Values.* London: Routledge & Kegan Paul. *17, 22, 27*

Peters, R. S. (1974) *Psychology and Ethical Development.* London: Allen and Unwin. *22, 26, 51*

Pirie, G. D. and Dalzell-Ward, A. J. (1962 and 1975) *A Textbook of Health Education*. London: Tavistock. *103*

Read, K. E. (1955) Morality and the concept of the person among the Gahuku-Gama. In J. Middleton (ed.) *Myth and Cosmos*. New York: Natural History Press, 185–229. *116*

Report of the Committee on Maladjusted Children (Underwood) (1955). London: HMSO. *70*

Robinson, J. A. T. (1963) *Honest to God*. London: SCM Press. *77*

Robinson, J. A. T. (1964) *Christian Morals Today*. London: SCM Press. *77, 110*

Rogers, A. (1961) (1962) Why teach history? The answer of fifty years I and II. *Educational Review 14(1)*: 10–20 and *14(2)*: 152–62. *107*

Rosenmayr, L. (1968) Towards an overview of youth sociology. *International Social Science Journal 20(2)*: 286–315. *126*

Sadler, M. E. (ed.) (1908) *Moral Instruction and Training in Schools*. London: Longmans Green. *61, 98, 101, 109*

Sartre, J-P. (1947) *Existentialism*. New York: Philosophical Library. *16*

Scheffler, I. (1965) *Conditions of Knowledge*. Chicago: Scott, Foresman. *111*

The School Health Service, 1908–1974 (1976) London: HMSO. *74*

Schools Council (1968) *Young School Leavers*. London: HMSO. *53, 79*

Schutz, A. (1970) *Reflections on the Problem of Relevance*. Newhaven: Yale University Press. *39, 42*

Schutz, A. (1971a) *Collected Papers: I*. The Hague: Nijhoff. *24, 37, 41*

Schutz, A. (1971b) *Collected Papers: II*. The Hague: Nijhoff. *33*

Schutz, A. and Luckmann, T. (1974) *The Structures of the Life-World*. London: Heinemann. *39*

Scott, J. F. (1971) *Internationalization of Norms: A Sociological Theory of Moral Commitment*. Englewood Cliffs: Prentice-Hall. *20*

Scull, A. T. (1975) From madness to mental illness: medical men as moral entrepreneurs. *Archives of European Sociology 16(2)*: 218–61. *61*

Selleck, R. J. W. (1968) *The New Education, 1870–1914*. London: Pitman. *109*

Selleck, R. J. W. (1972) *English Primary Education and the Progressives, 1914–1939*. London: Routledge & Kegan Paul. *69*

Simon, A. and Ward, L. O. (1972) Age, sex, history grades and moral judgements in comprehensive pupils. *Educational Research* *14(3)*: 191–4. *108*

Singer, P. (1972) Moral experts. *Analysis 32(4)*: 115–17. *112*

Stanley, M. (1973) The structures of doubt: reflections on moral intelligibility as a problem in the sociology of knowledge. In G. W. Remmling (ed.) *Towards a Sociology of Knowledge.* London: Routledge & Kegan Paul, 397–452. *24, 25, 28, 43, 122*

Sugarman, B. (1968) Moral education and the social structure of the school. *Journal of Curriculum Studies 1(1)*: 47–67. *89*

Szasz, T. S. (1961) *The Myth of Mental Illness,* New York: Harper & Row. *81*

Taylor, I., Walton, P. and Young, J. (1973) *The New Criminology.* London: Routledge & Kegan Paul. *27, 35*

Taylor, W. (1963) *The Secondary Modern School.* London: Faber. *93*

Trethewey, A. R. (1974) Social and educational influences on the definition of a subject: history in Victoria, 1850–1954. In P. W. Musgrave (ed.) *Contemporary Studies in the Curriculum.* Sydney: Angus and Robertson. *106, 107*

Tropp, A. (1957) *The School Teachers.* London: Heinemann. *68*

Turnbull, C. (1974) *The Mountain People.* London: Pan. *116*

Turner, R. H. (1976) The real self: from institution to impulse. *American Journal of Sociology 81(5)*: 989–1016. *76*

Ungoed-Thomas, J. (1972) *Our School: a handbook on the practice of democracy by secondary school pupils.* London: Longman. *94*

Wall, W. D. (1955) *Education and Mental Health.* Paris/London: UNESCO/Harrap. *85*

Watt, A. J. (1976) *Rational Moral Education. Melbourne:* Melbourne University Press. *121, 127*

Weinberg, I. (1967) *The English Public School.* New York: The Atherton Press. *62*

Westermarck, E. (1908) *The Origin and Development of the Moral Ideas* Vol. II. London: Macmillan. *17*

Wilson, J. (1969) *Education and the Concept of Mental Health.* London: Routledge & Kegan Paul. *29, 30*

Wilson, J. (1973) *The Assessment of Morality.* Slough: National Foundation for Educational Research. *21, 56, 117*

Wright, D. S. (1962) A comparative study of the adolescent's concepts of his parents and teachers. *Educational Review 14(3)*: 226–32. *126*

Wright D. (1971) *The Psychology of Moral Behaviour.* Harmondsworth: Penguin. *98*

Wright, D. and Cox, E. (1971) Changes in moral belief among sixth-form boys and girls over a seven Year period in relation to religious belief, age and sex differences. *British Journal of Social and Clinical Psychology* 10(4): 332–41. 51

Subject index

insanity – *see* mental illness
instability,
  moral and social, 120ff., 128
integrated studies, 108–9
internalization, 39
interpersonal relationships – *see*
  personal relationships

justice, concept of, 44, 46–8
justification, 33, 34

knowledge, 13, 21, 33, 38, 41,
  48, 56, 111

Labour Party, 72, 73, 74
Liberal Party, 72
lies, 34–6, 91
Local Government Act 1929, 71
lunacy – *see* mental illness
lying – *see* lies

maladjustment, 70, 81
medical profession,
  as moral educator, 30, 61, 68,
  70–1, 81, 82, 85, 87–8, 99–
  100, 101ff., 128 (*see also*
  health education, School
  Medical Service)
mental health, 27–31, 61, 70, 81,
  82, 83, 85, 86–7, 91, 103,
  119, 125, 128
Mental Health Act 1959, 82
mental illness, 27–31, 75, 79, 80
  and physical illness, 29–30
  and self-responsibility, 29–
  30, 81
  law in G.B., 82
middle class, 60, 61, 66, 74, 82,
  93
militarism, 42, 62, 65
Ministry of Health, 71, 102
mislearning, 30
moral action, 19–20, 22–3, 25,
  29, 43, 123, 128

moral change, 24, 26, 31, 33, 43,
  72ff., 87, 114, 121, 123, 128
  in growing up, 43–4, 56, 125
moral choice, 22–4, 25, 30, 32ff.,
  44, 57, 114, 125
  social-structural factor, 25–7,
  30, 36, 58, 73ff., 114ff. (*see
  also* moral decisions)
moral codes, 14–15, 22, 23, 26,
  29, 35, 37, 43, 49ff., 57, 60,
  74, 79, 87, 88, 92, 125, 127,
  128
  comparative studies, 115ff.
  sociological and philosophical
  differences, 121ff.
moral codes, plurality of – *see*
  pluralism
moral curriculum, 13–15, 33, 55,
  61ff., 65, 84, 87, 88, 119, 128
  and school curriculum, 13–
  14, 89–113, 125–7, 128
  in Russia, 117–19, 120
moral decisions, 21, 22, 33ff.,
  54, 57, 77, 87, 114, 127
  and commonsense, 25, 33, 37,
  41
  and weighting, 36–7, 41–2,
  56, 125
moral development, rates of,
  52
moral education, 29, 30, 33, 48,
  51, 57, 61, 75, 79, 83, 124ff.
  and school curriculum, 52ff.,
  83ff., 128–9
  and social class, 55, 66, 82–3,
  115
  children's views on, 51ff.
  comparison of societies,
  115ff., 124–5
  Durkheimian analysis, 18–19
  in extra-curricular activity,
  95–6
  in Scotland, 52–3
  non-cognitive factors, 19